WHEN I PRAYED FOR PATIENCE . . .
GOD LET ME HAVE IT

Jeanne Zornes
Psal 2:20

WHEN I PRAYED FOR PATIENCE . . . GOD LET ME HAVE IT!

JEANNE ZORNES

FOREWORD BY
JERRY B. JENKINS

Harold Shaw Publishers
Wheaton, Illinois

ISBN 0-87788-254-1

Edited by Vinita Hampton Wright

Cover design and illustration by David LaPlaca

Library of Congress Cataloging-in-Publication Data

Zornes, Jeanne, 1947-
    When I prayed for patience— : God let me have it! by Jeanne Zornes.
      p. cm.
    ISBN 0-87788-254-1
    1. Christian life. I. Title.
    BV4501.2.Z65 1995
    241'.4—dc20   95-1350
                                                              CIP

---

02 01 00 99 98 97 96 95

10 9 8 7 6 5 4 3 2 1

For Rich, Zachary, and Inga,
who endured mac-and-cheese
when writing clashed
with the dinner bell.

Contents

Foreword

Jeanne, an old friend and co-worker, told me about this book years ago. How exciting to see it finally come to fruition! It's just another example of patience and perseverance, the type of which its pages are full.

Jeanne had a lot of living and growing and changing to do during the manuscript's incubation period. I can't help but be grateful that she allowed it to progress in its own time. The finished product is the better for it, and thus will it be for you.

Earthy, pithy, practical, biblical, full of real stories, this is a book with lessons, but not from a teacher who holds them over your head. Rather, she comes alongside to say, "I've been there." She has. And it shows.

The years and the miles have left our brief friendship on a correspondence-only basis, but this book put Jeanne right back into the room with me. Welcome her to your reading spot, and growth will be the result.

God is in the details of life. Jeanne Zornes finds him, learns from him, and shares the wealth.

> Jerry B. Jenkins
> Author and
> Writer-in-Residence
> Moody Bible Institute, Chicago

Introduction

Buttonholed in the Garage

The real test of character is a building project.

If anything could go wrong, it will. And if anything *couldn't* go wrong, you can be sure it will anyway.

Or so I'm told by people who have built or remodeled—and survived to tell about it.

Like our neighbors, who turned their garage into a family room. Finishing up, they "cottage cheesed" the ceiling to match the rest of the house. But the new ceilings made the old look filthy. So they painted the rest of the ceilings. Which made the walls look dingy. Then came paint for the walls. Which made the rug look like it had endured twenty years of traffic in a greasy restaurant.

Then there were the empty-nesters who decided to redo half their house. "Never again," the wife moaned as I stopped one day by the wooden skeleton that had once been their kitchen, bathroom, and three bedrooms. And which, by that time, should have been ready to move in.

Then there's our house, one of three built on this street with the same floor plan. Tract homes are the composite of the lowest bidder, which means after a few years they tire out. The brown kitchen linoleum started peeling like an iron-on and the dark-stained cabinets showed the scars of over a decade of kicks and bumps. Plus I felt claustrophobic in this 11 x 15 room which sees all meals and snacks, most birthday parties, many crafts, computer work, and merciless Scrabble® games. So I decided to visually open up the space by painting the cabinets white and having white-and-blue flooring installed.

Painting the cabinets meant two coats of primer and two coats of enamel during the hottest week of summer. Ugh. I took a deep breath as we removed the cabinet doors and laid them on a tarp on the kitchen floor. My husband had to leave town, so I braced myself for solo painting on surfaces that showed every brush stroke.

One morning as I squatted over the cabinet doors smoothing on coat number two, the phone rang.

"Don't get excited when you see an ambulance come down the street," said my mother-in-law, who lives next door. "Dad fell and can't get up. He needs to go to the hospital."

Here I was, wearing clothes belonging to the rag bag, my hands and hair splattered sticky white, rushing next door to tell the ambulance guys which bedroom to go to while my mother-in-law comforted her husband.

My father-in-law's injuries were major league (a crushed first lumbar in a body already weakened by Parkinson's Disease), which meant multiple trips to the hospital. But we were too deep into the kitchen project to stop mid-stream. The flooring was next. Or so we thought.

We relieved the kitchen/dining/utility room of the stove, refrigerator, washer, dryer, table and chairs, computer desk, antique ice chest, and toilet, stuffing most of these items in the living room. Then my husband left for an out-of-town commitment.

My neighbor, knowing I was without appliances, offered to share a pizza order with me and my two children. I went out to the street to call for my 11-year-old son Zach, who'd gone for a bike ride this hot August night.

Zach limped home with a limp bike. He'd taken a turn too sharp and had become a human rocket. The helmet saved his head but the collision snapped his collar bone apart. This time I was the one headed to the hospital with a child who whimpered over every bump in the road.

We finally got our kitchen floor a few days later. And I was so happy that I didn't even think twice about crawling under the house, where black widows hide, to reattach the dryer vent. But that's another tale . . .

Home-improvement magazines never reveal the whole story. The tiny, ugly "before" and luxurious "after" shots don't tell all the "in-between" which drove the homeowners to the ragged edge of sanity. Maybe that's why we like to leaf through those magazines. We don't see all the agony of the process. We close our eyes to the dust, garbage, and inconvenience and bask in the elegance and comfort.

It's so much the same in our development as Christians. We want to accept Christ and have our spiritual houses immediately remodeled and cleaned up. We want instant readiness for heaven.

But holiness can't be hurried. Life is sometimes messy.

Like my garage. It's an example of spontaneous generation. Stuff just grows out of nothing. Sometimes I declare war, grab the broom, and attack.

One day I was in an extra feisty mood. Maybe it was my pre-schoolers getting to me. Zach and Inga had warred from the minute their sleeper footies hit rug. I should have dressed them in camouflage, not corduroy.

When my babies arrived nineteen months apart, several friendly advice-givers had predicted, "That close in age, they'll be such wonderful playmates for each other." Forget that!

As I brought them out to the garage with me, I figured one could ride the tricycle and the other wheel the pedal car while I worked. Instead, they drew lines for battle. I'd hardly turned my back when they were skirmishing over the tricycle.

I ignored their yowls of discontent as I jabbed the broom into obstinate corners. Then I heard a small piece of metal scuttle across the cement floor.

Stooping in curiosity, I found a little coat lapel button. Ten letters were its only message: PBPGINFWMY.

Translation, for those who missed that era of Christian-living seminars, when thousands of such buttons were passed out: "Please be patient. God is not finished with me yet."

What a day to get that reminder! Just when I think I can bring life under control, God reminds me who's in charge. I want life tidy and predictable. God allows it to become cluttered and unpredictable.

Sometimes I think I've already gone through enough. I should have arrived by now.

Job frustrations? Sure. Jobs in which I did things I wasn't trained to do. Jobs where I was bored or overwhelmed. Jobs under bosses with deserved reputations for being cantankerous. Others under leaders who didn't lead.

Housing frustrations? Singleness doesn't lend itself to palatial living quarters. One apartment had affordable rent—and a drug dealer for a neighbor. Another had narrow, high windows and a great view of the unmowed grass (a basement, if you didn't guess). And roommates—I had plenty. They moved through my life like a merry-go-round, propelled to other places by marriage or job changes.

Loneliness? I knew the depths when I was 31 and still single, and both my parents died within six months of each other. When I went back to graduate school to finish my master's degree, I felt utterly alone. How I missed writing or calling my mom and dad. How I wished they could have lived to see me march across the stage and get that long-sought-for degree.

Without them alive to share that moment, I skipped the commencement ceremony. Borrowing an academic gown and hood, I asked a friend to snap my picture in front of Old Main, for posterity, I guess. But my aloneness hurt.

Uncertainties? I'd anticipated my graduate training as a fast ticket to the job market. More than a thousand miles from "home" (or at least from the storage unit holding my "stuff"), I swamped the post office with resumes and waited . . . and waited. A job finally came, just three heart-stopping days before I had to vacate my housing.

In time came marriage. And children. Just when we start to snuggle down into a bed of self-righteous satisfaction, God has a way of waking us up. God's wisdom mixed an old bachelor (finally, at thirty-six, tiring of boxed meat pies and bargain burgers) and an old maiden (age thirty-four, a specialist in five-day tuna casserole). Then he added children with opposite temperaments and a variety of other people and their problems.

This is how God builds people: one brick at a time, and foundations and walls before the fancy stuff. We may wait years to enjoy the finishing touches. As I grow older, I'm starting to understand the wisdom of God's construction process. There's so much truth to the observation of Paul Billheimer:

> If God's net purpose in saving an individual is just to get him to heaven, He would probably take him to glory immediately. But God wants to prepare him for rulership in an infinite universe that demands character. Progress in sanctification, in the development of God-

like character and agape love, is impossible without tribulation and chastisement.[1]

That's why I've known difficult jobs, frustrating people, and stretching times. They've allowed me to see myself as God sees me. They've shown me a person-in-progress with a weakness to put "me" first—before God or others. Life's difficulties have revealed a stubborn spirit that demands "Why?" instead of simply accepting that God knows why.

I've learned I can't pray for patience and expect God to solve the problems immediately. Sometimes he may choose to do so. But more often, he will use those difficult times to push up the ceiling of my intolerance, to push out the walls of my prejudices, and to muck out the garbage of my grudges.

Getting remodeled by the Creator of the Universe is no picnic. But it's necessary if I am to become the person he wants me to be.

During this lifelong construction process, we're sometimes unaware of the changes taking place.

The other day a friend and I were musing how we don't feel so "old." Sure, we rub oils on our wrinkles, pluck out those gray hairs until they come too fast, and wear shoulder pads to pull attention away from our expanding middles. But inside, in our minds, we think of ourselves as ten or so years behind our bodies.

"Hey, I'm not that different from years ago," my friend laughed.

But I was sobered by our discussion. "I am," I countered. "I can think of a lot of things I said and did which I now regret. But God's been reconstructing a lot of areas of my personality and spirit. I'm not the same person I used to be."

And I'm thankful for it. That's why I can share, with re-morse but with gratefulness for God's mercy, some of those growing pains. That's why I can ask you to be patient, be-cause we all need to give each other that growing space as we seek to become more like Christ.

We pray this in order that you may live a life worthy of the Lord and may please him in every way . . . so that you may have great endurance and patience.—Colossians 1:10-11

1

Did Somebody Yell "Patience"?

Sometimes there just aren't the right words to say what we mean.

I remember one such time in Mexico City. As a mission journalist, I was helping cover the international meeting of mission executives.

I was an unfortunate choice.

When you go to Mexico, you should speak Spanish. That means more than "sí," "no," "taco" "baño" (bathroom), and "agua" (water). Yes, I took Spanish in high school; but because of a conflict with orchestra, I got plunked in the bonehead language class. After ten years I'd forgotten much of even that.

So here I was, a green gringo from headquarters in southern California. My adventurous editor decided to maximize the benefits of my presence and sent me with some returning workers to the southern jungles to interview some missionaries. Assignment done, I flew back to Mexico City.

One problem. Nobody was there to pick me up.

I'd learned enough about the culture to know I shouldn't climb into the first taxi, especially since I looked "rico" enough to command a good fare. I should bargain. So, wandering among the anxious drivers, I showed them the paper telling my destination.

"Sí," said one driver hungry enough to meet my counter-offer. As he started ramming through Mexico City's Judges 17:6 traffic ("Everyone did what was right in his own eyes"), I decided I'd end up either at mission headquarters or in heaven. However, I thought I'd better explain a little more thoroughly where I hoped to arrive. "Está circa de instituto de lunatico," I said in my fractured Spanish, remembering that a mental hospital was just over the fence from the mission grounds.

My driver looked at me strangely and eventually pulled into the driveway of the state mental asylum.

I experienced a similar frustration in writing this book about patience. I knew where I wanted to end up, but I struggled with the right words for the process and destination.

The English word "patience" shows up about forty times in Scripture. But it's on every page in its many different faces. Our language limits the richness of this attribute.

Galatians 5:22 calls patience a "fruit of the spirit." But it can't be pigeonholed into one corner of our spiritual lives. It's interlaced with the other fruits, for a patient person is also loving, joyful, peaceful, kind, good, faithful, gentle and self-controlled. It's more than a "cool spirit" or the ability to remain calm in turmoil. It's greater than the passive state of waiting or resigning oneself to circumstances. Instead, it's stalwart stuff described by words like *longsuffering, forbearance, endurance, perseverance,* and *trust.* Biblical patience is active, tough, and vibrant. It moves toward certain life goals.

There's a spiritual progression inherent in the five biblical terms for patience. We move from dealing with life's daily annoyances to anticipating a finished character's profound rewards in eternity.

There are no instant Perfect People. All our lives have spiritual clutter. But as God trains us in these qualities, little by little he takes care of that clutter. As he does, we learn to love and worship him more.

That is why I wrote this book—to help put names and perspective on life's troubles and questions, to see the sense of them, and to thank God for them.

A Quick Preview of the Pages Ahead

Longsuffering (covered in chapters 2 and 3) is the quality that keeps you going when you're abused or provoked. Zach, at four, screeched about criminal trespass as Inga (two and a half) slithered into his room and snitched a favorite truck. Then Inga sirened to my side, charging, "Zach pushed me!"

Thinking about "suffering long" reminds me of a friend whose résumé I typed when she was job-hunting. I was struck by her long list of short-term jobs. Then I pieced together her problem: she was a quitter when things got tough.

Forbearance (chapters 4 and 5) is the ability to bear with the shortcomings of others—and of ourselves. What better illustration than first-time parents hovering over their newborn. We chalked up to "parenting" all those squeaks and squawks that summoned us to remedy hunger, thirst, mess, heat, or boredom. We loved our little crib residents to pieces, even when they kept us awake from 3 to 6 A.M.

A couple years later, those babies-turned-toddlers learned their own painful lessons in coping with selfishness and personal flaws. "Inga doesn't play nice," pouted Zach, at three.

"Remember, she's still a baby," I reasoned, trying to distract him to an activity with less opportunity for conflict.

Someday they'll understand that love covers a multitude of sins (1 Pet. 4:8). I hope they learn that lesson well and become people who make and *keep* friends. If their marriages involve some storms, I want them willing to work things out so their love is renewed, not destroyed.

Endurance (chapters 6 and 7) holds up under the circumstances that try us. Or as William Barclay put it, "Endurance is not just the ability to bear a hard thing, but to turn it into glory."[1] This word is used in today's conversations, but we can learn more about what it means by exploring its biblical roots.

At eighteen months, Inga had difficulty enduring the Law of the Crib. Delusions of liberation sent her swan-diving off the top of the rails. One dive at three in the morning ended with her biting completely through her lip, sending us to the emergency room.

Endurance is hanging tough when the crib is boring and confining. I see it in people who cheerfully cope with their adverse circumstances. Hazel, now in her mid-eighties, has spent a decade on crutches, bearing much pain because of a hip surgery gone wrong. Yet she's always upbeat and more eager to hear others' news than relate her aches.

I have a lot to learn here! One time I went through a siege of migraines. My children were playing "house" and I overheard Inga instructing Zach, "You be the daddy. I'll be the mommy and I have a headache, so don't bother me!" If only the real thing were as easy as play. If only Romans 12:12— "patient in affliction"—were a cinch!

Perseverance (chapters 8 and 9) is a sister trait to endurance. Perseverance not only holds up in trying circumstances, but is headed toward a goal in the process. Zach, now eleven, will spend hours squatting on the floor with his big box of Legos®. He has a vision of the contraption he's building—usually some sort of space-age transport. That keeps him patiently sorting through all the gravel-size pieces to find just the right one.

I see the same holding-on in a woman who came to Christ from a life bruised by alcoholism and drugs. There's still "clutter" in her life, but she's moving forward with God's best purposes as her heart's desire.

And I've seen the failure to persevere. I've cried for, and with, young women who gave up persevering in God's command to remain pure while single. Yielding to premarital intimacy, they found themselves pregnant and abandoned, their lives forever scarred by that lapse in hanging on for God's best.

Jesus knows our weaknesses, our tendency to give up. Yet he longs to assure us of his steadfast love: "As the Father has loved me, so have I loved you. Now remain in my love" (John 15:9). His love, his incredible compassion for us despite our failures, can help us persevere as we keep our eyes on him.

In the end, as a result of developing these many qualities, we come to genuine *trust*, which has learned to rely on God's character and promises and waits for God's will in God's time. How hard that can be! Yet the psalmist urged, "Commit your way to the Lord; trust in him and he will do this" (Ps. 37:5).

"No cookie until you eat your yogurt," I told my children as pre-schoolers. "Brian can come play after your nap." "We'll have to stay inside and look at the snow until your earache is better." They bristled at Mom's agenda. Yet they were learning to trust, to accept others' wiser priorities. Ultimately, I pray, they'll learn to say yes to all of God's plan. It's a profound lesson, one I am still learning when life is so difficult to understand.

Right now we're dealing with the dying process. My husband's father, a retired minister, has Parkinson's Disease, an intruder leeching him of mobility and mind. Moving from one room to another is an arduous task; his thinking is scrambled. When I stay with him to give his wife a break from caretaking, I silently ask why we can't get whisked to heaven like Enoch, whom God simply "took," or like Elijah, who went in the thrill of chariots of fire. Then God turns around and asks me to *trust*—that in his glorious plan all this will be made clear.

Over the past few years that lesson has sunk even deeper into my spirit as our lives intersect with those going through incredible personal pain.

- People struggling through unemployment or financial reversals, or unable to conquer spending habits.

- Friends and relatives who've reeled under the shock of divorce or marital unfaithfulness.

- The precious couple who watched their son choose homosexuality, then die inch by inch of AIDS.

- Another friend, with a child whose cancer has no cure.

- The couple struggling with infertility while a relative chooses abortion.

- The young woman who waited years to conceive, only to have two babies die in her womb.

■ The parents whose son became addicted to alcohol and drugs.

■ The friend who maimed one wife emotionally, and killed a second wife.

■ Another who yielded to a thoughtless moment of sexual indiscretion.

Some of these problems continue. So do the prayers—and tears. But through them God reminds me he's not finished with me—or any of us—yet.

My children are good illustrations of that truth. When I see them battle over each others' toys, I think of times when we war in grown-up ways over things or positions. When my little ones do their temper tantrum dances, I'm reminded of my own spiritual rough spots and tendency to demand things of God.

We've all snickered over the saying, "I want patience and I want it right now!" When my children start whining their demands, they'll often hear from Mom or Dad, "You don't always get what you want." But God *does* want to build in us a character that is strong, kind, and purposeful. As we learn to show grace to others, to accept ourselves, and to bear up under adversity, we'll gain in increasing measure all the golden qualities of Christlike character.

Many of us have cluttered spiritual garages. Our actions and words reveal character that, on some days, seems to be still in the blueprint stage. But we all have the how-to manual for putting order to the mess and allowing God to get the construction going. God's Word teaches us how to accept each difficulty, each hardship, as part of the process of learning to live for Jesus. Romans 15:4 says that "through endurance and the encouragement of the Scriptures we might have hope."

This book will share that hope. My prayer is that it will lead you to a life more characterized by faith, hope, and love.

Something to Build On

1. One of the Greek words translated "patience" in the New Testament is *hupomone,* which means "an abiding under." It has both a passive and active sense. The passive sense involves endurance. The active sense of *hupomone* denotes persistence or perseverance. What aspect is touched in these scriptures? *Ausdauer*

> 2 Corinthians 12:12 *active*
> Hebrews 12:7 *passive*
> James 1:12 *passive*
> 1 Peter 2:20b *passive*
> Luke 8:15 *passive*
> Romans 2:7 *active*
> Hebrews 12:1 *passive*

2. Holiness has been called both a process and a progression. What does 2 Peter 1:5-8 suggest? Where would you put yourself in that "learning list"—what stage are you at? *process*

3. Read 1 Thessalonians 1:2-3. What elements does Paul consider praiseworthy in their lives? Define each in your own words and give examples.

4. Set aside ten 3x5 cards for memory work based on this study. After each chapter you'll be offered a key verse. Post it where you'll see it every day and let it grow in your heart. For

9

chapter 1, this verse is a reminder to grow more Christlike:

Therefore, as God's chosen people, holy and dearly loved, clothe yourselves with compassion, kindness, humility, gentleness and patience.—Colossians 3:12

If you stumble in safe country, how will you manage in the thickets by the Jordan?—Jeremiah 12:5b

2

Moving beyond Murphy

Growing through Annoyances

Some days you want to erase yourself from life.

Like the morning I overslept. For good reason, mind you. I'd been up and down all night with sick babies.

As I stumbled out of bed, I passed by the mirror and wondered who was that crazy lady with the punk-rock hairdo. Forget those commercials in which an immaculately groomed female eases into wakefulness to the soothing aroma of coffee.

I ripped a brush through my hair and then grabbed the bawling, teething, diaper-soggy baby en route to the kitchen.

There I was greeted by an invasion of ants, feasting under the toddler's high chair. I hastily stamped them off to ant heaven and then reached into the refrigerator for eggs. As I shifted the baby to my other hip, I was thrown off-balance.

11

Guess what happened to the eggs. Yes, sunny-side up, uncooked, on the floor.

About that time, in bounced Happy Husband, the physical education teacher in a rush to get to school. I looked at his feet and wished I could disappear. My sin had found me out.

A few days earlier, wearing his almost-new tennis shoes, my husband Rich had been inspired to rototill our still muddy garden. I tossed the now brown tennies into the next dark clothes wash. I didn't count on a conspiracy by a pair of red pants in that load. Out came pink tennies, which would be okay for a phys. ed. teacher—who is female. Hoping Rich wouldn't miss them, I shoved the pink shoes into the darkest corner of his closet. It wasn't dark enough. "Hey," he chirped, "what happened to my shoes?"

The Universal Laws of Murphy

Murphy was right. Three laws govern the universe:
1. Nothing is as easy as it looks.
2. Everything takes longer than you think it will.
3. If anything can go wrong, it will.

Life has its way of throwing monkey wrenches in the gears of all our best plans. We're tempted to think that if we were just a bit more organized, or had another job or another piece of equipment, or could work with somebody who had his act together—well, all these problems wouldn't happen.

But life isn't tidy. And that's good. Inconveniences (usually the type inspired by Murphy's Laws) and injustices have their place. They're part of our spiritual training program.

Internationally-known Bible teacher J. I. Packer puts it this way:

Patience means living out the belief that God orders everything for the spiritual good of his children. Patience does not just grin and bear things, stoic-like, but accepts them cheerfully as therapeutic workouts planned by a heavenly trainer who is resolved to get you up to full fitness.

Patience, therefore, treats each situation as a new opportunity to honor God in a way that would otherwise not be possible, and acts accordingly. Patience breasts each wave of pressure as it rolls in, rejoicing to prove that God can keep one from losing his or her footing.[1]

That's the message implicit in Jeremiah 12:5. The weeping prophet was having a pity party. He'd been telling his countrymen that God wanted changed lives, not religious ritual. But they didn't care, and continued on in their wickedness and prosperity. Not only did they spurn his preaching, they also plotted his death (see 11:18-23). Jeremiah had enough of this scene.

But God had an answer. This was just the warmups.

If you have raced with men on foot and they have worn you out, how can you compete with horses? *Jeremiah 12:5a*

Jeremiah was panting to the finish line of the 100-meter dash. But the Kentucky Derby—man versus super-horse—was ahead. Now, people he hardly knew were giving him a hard time. Soon, he'd face the king, the court, and the priests at Jerusalem. Their opposition would be incredibly difficult.

If you stumble in safe country, how will you manage in the thickets by the Jordan? *Jeremiah 12:5b*

Jeremiah's current landscape was like Montana Big Sky country. But he'd soon enter Jordan's jungles. Jeremiah knew enough geography to grasp God's symbolism. The Jordan river flows through some bottomlands so wooded that at times you can't see the river. Hot, full of thick undergrowth, it's the haunt of wild animals.

"Toughen up," God was saying. "I've got a bigger job ahead for you."

That's the same message God speaks to us in life's Murphyisms. He allows us little tests to tone up our spiritual muscle. He uses the dailyness of life to sculpt us into holy people. He takes our *im*patience and twists the whines out of it to turn us into people who can say *"I'm* patient."

Frankly, I think this is the arena of spiritual growth where God delights in showing us his sense of humor. The unpredictable, perturbing potholes we encounter in this journey show how original he can be. Like these from our family's Murphy's Law Memoirs:

■ The toast always lands jelly-side down.

■ The dinner guest was extolling the freshness of a salad from our garden. In the next bite he found a green worm.

■ It was a short-on-cash month. So the washer gasped its last (on Friday, seven loads to go), the oven's heating element blasted a hole in itself, and the car's water pump fizzled to death.

■ The fretful baby was finally down for her nap when a confident salesman with a heavy thumb pressed the doorbell.

■ Sneakers (underwear, coats, you-name-it) went on sale the day *after* our purchases.

■ You have a headache no aspirin could cure, but your neighbor has the flu to end all flus. She needs to unload her non-stop preschoolers—guess where.

■ You're fighting a reputation for always being late to church. This week you're determined to make the 8:30 service. You plop baby in the playpen—freshly powdered, frocked, and bonneted—while you run to the bathroom to brush your teeth and pull a brush through your hair. On the return run, you're stuffing your arms in your coat when you sniff manure from the playpen and notice telltale brown splotches on her once-pristine tights.

What's a person to do? Just what J. I. Packer said—to accept these situations *cheerfully* as therapeutic workouts planned by a heavenly trainer. Post on the mirror those marching orders from Philippians 4:4: "Rejoice in the Lord always."

And learn to laugh. People like me, who want everything right for the sake of our reputations (go ahead and snicker), find this a hard thing to do. But laughter defuses the poison of negative reactions. Listen to Donald Demaray, in *Laughter, Joy and Healing:*

We all suffer temptation to succumb to negatives. But humor is a great antidote, emancipating us to live above the trivial. . . . The more one believes in the sovereignty of God, the greater the freedom to enjoy God's world and even to laugh at life's contradictions.[2]

Some Hall of Fame-ers

Washington state is actually two states: the "wet side" and the "dry side." The Cascade Mountains split the state, acting like a big fence that keeps most of the rain over in places like Seattle, where the city symbol should be an umbrella. We live on the "dry side" of the state, where Douglas firs are generally replaced by sagebrush. Only irrigation has made the dry side inhabitable. But at least we don't have webbed feet like our wet-side neighbors.

When our friends Phil and Darlene moved to the "wet side" to take a new pastorate, they literally had a water baptism of trouble. The Saturday their family of five moved into the tiny parsonage, they barely managed to set up beds and put out Sunday's clothes before collapsing.

"I was so tired and sore I thought a nice warm bath would feel so good," Darlene recalls. "I began to draw my bath, and surprise! About 25 per cent water pressure or less! Fifteen minutes later I had about four inches of water in the tub!"

The shower wasn't much better. It emitted a fine mist (the type you see in produce sections of high-tech grocery stores) that was disastrously affected by someone turning on the kitchen faucet. They waited ten minutes for the washing machine to fill for half a load.

There were tears as the children started in new, strange schools. Then their oldest, unaccustomed to driving in rain, collided with a moving van six blocks from home. The family came down with colds. Phil got a cough so bad it threw his back out. Their son developed pneumonia. Darlene, directing two choirs, lost her voice.

One weekend they went away to a mission festival. Sure, it was rainy, but they didn't expect to come home Saturday night to eight inches of water in the basement, spoiling mattresses and boxes of life's "stuff."

As the basement started draining, the furnace motor, submerged in water, burned out and filled the house with smoke. The flood also found their cat Frisky's litter box. Woe upon woe, Frisky also had a urinary infection. She refused to go out in the rain and decided her only other option was the kitchen floor.

The next day, Sunday, found them mist-showering by candlelight and shivering in the feeble warmth of space heaters. They'd already invited another family over to watch the Super Bowl. So they went ahead with Plan A, plus lots of blankets.

"Just like the stadium," Darlene remarked.

Ready for more? Their station wagon leaked, the family's beloved cat got so sick she needed surgery, then went into respiratory arrest. The vet called to report Frisky's demise just ten minutes before Phil and Darlene were supposed to teach a class on loving your child. That's hard to do when your youngest is sobbing over the loss of her kitty.

They went to a minister's conference and came home to pipes broken in the basement and four inches of wet down there. When Phil and another man tried to fix them, they only succeeded in breaking more. Now, there was no cold water in the bathroom, except for a trickle in the toilet, and no Sunday morning showers. Monday, new pipes were installed, but then the water heater rebelled.

Those first watery months also brought disappointment further up the adversity scale when a land deal for a new church building project fell through, along with the family's plans to move into a more spacious mobile home with water pipes that worked.

But all these troubles were the foot races before bigger challenges.

One was the church building project. The old church sold, and the congregation struggled to pull together while worshipping temporarily in rented halls. Seemingly perfect property deals crashed before they finally got the green light to buy and build. Then came all the decisions and complications of putting up a new church.

Another challenge was a deepening understanding of people. The give-and-take of ministry pulled them into learning greater dimensions of grace and forbearance with difficult people. They tasted more tears and learned greater compassion as they came alongside more people hurt by crime and abuse.

Finally would come a difficult departure, a cautious move into new jobs, and health problems requiring lifestyle adjustments.

As Phil and Darlene look back, they realize how their foot races became horse races—a move from annoyances to life's seeming impossibilities.

For many years, Darlene clung to the promise expressed in a devotional book a friend gave her when they moved to the "wet" side. The friend underlined this passage, more appropriately than she could have ever realized:

Remember, that wherever you are, you are put there by God; and by the reaction of your life to the circumstances around you, you will fulfill God's purpose, as long as you keep in the light as God is in the light.[3] *That is so true, but I failed miserable today—turn over 8/12/95*

"It's easy to get caught up in the 'if-onlies,' " Darlene says. "But those years of change and challenge taught us that God places us where he wants, in the circumstances that are best for us at the moment. If we accept them with the right attitude, then we can make it with smiles on our faces."

Smiling Lessons

Smiles brighten life. They brighten dark corners—or so we learn from the life of Ina Dudley Ogdon. She gave us that phrase, "brighten the corner where you are."

Around the turn of the century, she was on the verge of a shining career with the Chautauqua cultural circuit as an author/poet. But she found herself instead staying at home to care for her invalid father.

Ina struggled for a time. Caring for a sick old man wasn't quite the same as bowing to the applause of a thrilled audience. But as God led her to his perspective on her trial, she gave it voice in this song:

> Do not wait until some deed of greatness you may do—
> Do not wait to shed your light afar.
> To the many duties ever near you now be true;
> Brighten the corner where you are.[4]

Murphy-isms will continue to kick aside our best plans. But when we see these annoyances and inconveniences as part of God's training program, then we can truly brighten the corners where we are.

Then we'll be ready when Murphy's mud puddles become the thickets of the Jordan—or worse.

In the next chapter, Psalm 37 will guide us through those thickets that sometimes throw us into the deepest despair.

Something to Build On

1. Read Hebrews 12:7-11. What does it suggest comes as a result of hardship? *It yields the peaceable fruit of righteousness.*

2. What phrases appear more than once in Psalm *✓5+11* 42? How could you apply them to dealing with discouragement?

3. <u>Sometimes we can be so proud that we refuse</u> <u>to go through an inconvenience that could</u> <u>bring honor to God.</u> How was this true of Naaman when he sought a cure for his leprosy? (See 2 Kings 5:1-15, noting verses 11-12.)

    Refuse to help kids w/their luggage— wheelbarrow BLBC Summer '95

4. Even after his discipline in the whale, Jonah had a selfish side that pouted over annoyances. What lessons can be gleaned from Jonah 4:5-11?

God gets His way no matter what. It's best to do it right the 1st time.

But grow in the grace and knowledge of our Lord and Savior Jesus Christ. To him be glory, both now and forever! Amen.
—2 Peter 3:18

For it is commendable if a man bears up under the pain of unjust suffering because he is conscious of God.—1 Peter 2:19

3

Going Forward in Reverse

Bearing with Adversity

The car in our garage is a monument to a hard lesson learned one unforgettable September night.

My husband was out of town, so I'd fielded all the mom, dad, and referee duties. I'll admit, I was getting a bit grouchy. Also an August cold had turned into an earache.

But it was my son's ninth birthday. Nothing should spoil that. So we arranged to have his best buddy go with us to the local drive-in to see a Disney dog cartoon.

It was a little after ten when I dropped the friend off at his house, just down the block. I got back in the car, put my foot firmly on the brake, and shifted gears to reverse.

In a nightmare of seconds, the car screamed in a semi-circle back into the next-door neighbor's front yard, glancing off the electrical power box between the properties. The car stopped just short of the neighbor's house, the bumper bending an iron rod staking a young tree. Somehow, I got the shift stick out of reverse.

But the neighborhood had plunged into darkness.

Shaken and horrified, I realized I'd put my foot on the accelerator, not the brake. So here we sat in the neighbor's yard, my children crying and me numb with fear.

Had just a few things been different—like the neighbor's car parked, as usual, in the path of my high-speed backing— I could have injured or killed my own children. As it was, only the power box and the car bumper suffered damage.

That fast trip in reverse taught me about more than the effectiveness of seat belts. For one thing, I saw my self-sufficiency threatened. I was trying so hard to be Super Mom, to give my son a memorable birthday (boy, was it memorable!), trying to keep things going with Dad gone, trying to carry on despite the annoying throb in my ear. Now I had the first accident to smudge my insurance record.

But then my irritation changed to repentance. I realized that only the hand of God had prevented a worse accident. I was reminded of how these children—as demanding as they can be sometimes—are infinitely precious to me and to their heavenly Father.

That accident was another lesson in longsuffering—in learning to see the long perspective on suffering.

Attitudes That Go Forward, Not Backward

When I emerge from difficult situations with meekness, not anger, I know I've gone forward, not backward. Meekness shows that I've learned submissiveness and obedience to God. It is evidence that I'm learning to replace pride and independence with the attitude of someone who knows her limitations and is willing to learn and be helped. No wonder

Jesus highlighted this trait in the beatitudes: "Blessed are the meek, for they will inherit the earth" (Matt. 5:5).

In that beatitude Jesus was actually quoting from Psalm 37:11: "The meek will inherit the land and enjoy great peace." The entire psalm deals with going forward when life is in reverse. Its focus is the reaction God wants us to have when faced with injustice and inequities.

The writer of the psalm, David, considered a righteous person's insecurity when the wicked seem to prosper. David surely knew such anxiety when pursued by the crazed King Saul. But his experience continues to speak to us when life seems to treat us unfairly and when adversity stretches our longsuffering nearly to breaking points.

The psalm wastes no words as it opens: "Do not fret because of evil men or be envious of those who do wrong" (Psa. 37:1). The word "fret" is a good picture of our confusion and impatience. Envision something that can vex, grate, irritate, corrode, rub, chafe, or wear away. For example, a stream can fret a channel. God is saying, "Don't get all torn up inside when things seem to go well for others, but not for you. Don't get upset when you see evil people getting all the good breaks." Instead, we are to get preoccupied with God. Get the long view—eternity's perspective. God knows the destiny of the wicked:

For like the grass they will soon wither, like green plants they will soon die away. (v. 2)

But their swords will pierce their own hearts, and their bows will be broken. (v. 15)

I have seen a wicked and ruthless man flourishing like a green tree in its native soil, but he soon passed away and was no more; though I looked for him, he could not be found. (vv. 35-36)

God says to turn to him for instructions in acquiring a quiet spirit. He's got the solution for indignation and envy. It comes with five commands:

- Trust

- Delight

- Commit

- Be still

- Turn from anger

Trust

"Trust in the Lord and do good" says Psalm 37:3a. We're to seek safety in the Lord himself. As 19th-century English preacher Charles H. Spurgeon expressed it:

> Faith cures fretting. Sight is cross-eyed, and views things only as they seem; hence her envy. Faith has clearer optics to behold things as they are; hence her peace.[1]

Trust says, "Okay, Lord, I can't see the reason. My glasses are all smudged up with my problems. I'll believe that you are in control." The other part of that command puts our trust to action. We're to "do good," to actively obey.

The rest of that verse elaborates: "dwell in the land and enjoy safe pasture." God doesn't want us running away from our problems, from the very pressures that will help us grow. He says *dwell*. Live there, learn there.

That came home to me when my mother died and my father added my name as a signatory to his banking. He showed me his will and financial papers, taught me how to open the family safe, and indicated that he wanted me to handle his affairs when he died. I guess he felt my older sister had enough to do, busy with the demands of a family and business.

My insides churned as he did this. I hurt so deeply over losing Mother that I didn't want to think of him dying, too. But I knew—and he knew—that life held no guarantees. A two-time heart attack survivor, he'd collapsed at church less than a year earlier. A nurse sitting behind him had revived him.

Six months after he'd explained his business affairs, a phone call reached me in graduate school more than a thousand miles away. Another heart attack was his last, and my life would never be the same. Dropping out of my studies, I moved home to do what Dad had requested of me.

Awash in grief, I struggled through all the financial rigamarole necessary to satisfy creditors, courts, and the government. I lived in my parents' cluttered, memory-tugging house as I sorted junk, painted, scrubbed, weeded, and mowed. Then came seven garage sales: strangers picking over my parents' possessions, haggling about prices.

All the time I wondered why it had to take so *long*. Sometimes old high school friends came to the garage sales. I looked at their children and heard them talk about their families and homes. Here I was, in my thirties, still single, and rootless. My job of "settling affairs" would dissolve what had been my earthly security. I felt as though I was in a deep, wide pool, just treading water, unable to swim to shore.

But God said, "Dwell in the land and enjoy safe pasture" (v. 3). A church home had always been a priority for me. And so as soon as I could, I linked up with a body of believers. I deliberately went to a smaller church where my presence would be noticed. It would have been too easy—and too spiritually dangerous—to slip through the cracks of a larger church. Soon Sundays became a time of safety as I worked through grieving's physical and emotional demands. When I cried, people understood. One woman my age, who had recently buried her brother, cared for me in a genuine way.

Delight

"Delight yourself in the Lord," says verse 4, "and he will give you the desires of your heart."

My grieving pushed me into the Bible as never before. A friend gave me a Bible in the newest translation and I read it through in three months. Then I made a return trip, discovering even more consolation and promises.

It became natural to tell others how those Bible verses leaped off the page at me. Intimacy with Scripture led to intimacy with God. I started to realize what David's chief musician, Asaph, meant in another psalm:

Whom have I in heaven but you? And earth has nothing I desire besides you. My flesh and my heart may fail, but God is the strength of my heart and my portion forever. *Psalm 73:25-26*

Needing an outlet beyond the legal paperwork and garage sales, I signed up for class guitar lessons through the local adult education program. As those I-IV-V chords became less mysterious and my picking patterns more comfortable, I filled the empty, lonely hours with singing "Gentle Shepherd," "Be Thou My Vision," and other songs that expressed my soul.

I realized why Paul and Silas turned to music that night as they sat in the jail at Philippi. They knew Adversity—with a capital *A*. Preaching Christ had not brought glory and fame. Seized and beaten, they were tossed into prison. They had plenty of reason to "fret because of evil men." Instead, they ended up "praying and singing hymns to God" (Acts 16:25). They redirected their emotional responses to the Lord, delighting in his company. Then came the earthquake and their release. Oh, the joy from having *him* as Joy! God gave them the desire of their hearts.

Commit

The third command, "Commit your way to the Lord" (v. 5), expresses the idea of yielding difficulties to God. The Hebrew word for *commit* literally means "to roll," like getting rid of a burden.

It's like workers I saw on a banana plantation. One set of workers cut down the man-size stalks containing dozens of green bananas. Then others would bear these across their shoulders and back to a central loading place. Gently they'd roll these burdens off onto cushioned trailers.

God says we need to bring him our entire heavy, unmanageable burden, and just roll it onto his strong shoulders.

When we trust him with that load, he wants to show the excellence of his plan. The "commit" command embraces this promise:

> Trust in him and he will do this: He will make your righteousness shine like the dawn, the justice of your cause like the noonday sun. (vv. 5b-6)

When we turn our situations over to God, he'll work out the results. They'll be as obvious to others as bright sunlight. And God's kindness and power will emerge in the sight of those who observe our lives.

Be Still

The hardest part of waiting is "just before." Just before you see the answer. Just before you're ready to give up. Just before it all breaks open, and you understand.

"Be still before the Lord," says verse 7, "and wait patiently for him." This means accepting God's holy timetable. Spurgeon remarked, "Time is nothing to Him. Let it be nothing to thee. God is worth waiting for. He never is before his time. He never is too late."[2]

Settling my parents' affairs took ten months of work and waiting. Sale of the house, during a time of crippling interest rates, kept me in a holding pattern much longer than I wanted.

Yet God was at work. A Christian lawyer nudged me back to school, urging me to trust God for the last of my expenses. The house didn't sell until I'd graduated. But oddball jobs kept food on the table and I graduated with my tuition bill paid in full.

Turn from Anger

The only negative instruction in Psalm 37 regarding how we deal with adversity is verse 8: "Refrain from anger and turn from wrath." When we're disturbed by the seeming prosperity of evil, we're apt to respond with some version of anger, such as envy, indignation, or verbal abuse.

My initial reaction after the car accident was anger toward my husband and children. I wanted to blame them for the circumstances that caused the accident. Then I was angry at myself for my stupidity. But my anger didn't do any good.

The same was true when my parents died. I slogged through a whole cesspool of anger and self-pity, wondering why I got stuck with all the work when I was on the verge of really getting on with life. I was miserable inside and miserable to be around.

When it got down to the bottom line, I was angry at God. I argued that I didn't need these additional troubles. I had enough. Couldn't he see that?

As the anger oozed out of my heart, I was taken right back to Romans 12:21: "Do not be overcome by evil, but overcome evil with good." I've always thought that verse deserves a typographical error on that last word: "Overcome evil with God."

When faced with evil—that of circumstances or of difficult people—we need to turn right back to the Author of good.

Getting angry with circumstances won't change them. It's like kicking a wall. You'll only stub or break your toes. Getting angry with people won't improve the situation either. Jesus gave tough advice: "Love your enemies, do good to those who hate you" (Luke 6:27). It's hard, but it makes so much sense. When you do love them, you won't carry the burden of having complicated the problem with unloving behavior.

Listen to James Bishop, founder of the South Indian Bible Institute:

> The world is full of people who believe in standing up for their rights, and the world is in an awful mess. Self-renunciation is the prime factor in the successful pursuit of peace. A glad willingness to suffer wrong rather than to do wrong will cure most troubles in a community or institution.
>
> This is not to say we should be guilty of a slavish subserviency. We are to be subservient, not to circumstances, not to men, but to God. Our surrender is never to stop short of being unto *Him*. It is to be an active, aspiring surrender. The outcome which His working produces is to be our goal. We can furnish the human agency for His working, but only His working can produce the desired results.[3]

Our car was driveable after that heart-stopping trip in reverse. I walked my children home, and a neighbor stayed with them while I talked to police.

Later, as I eased the car home to the garage, I thought how it could have been dangerously impaled on that electrical box. Instead, the car was knocked away. God was there!

After cups of cocoa, prayers, and much cuddling and rocking, I finally got the children to sleep. But I tossed in my bed for hours. My husband was nowhere near a phone; and even if he had been, he couldn't have done anything.

Finally I got up and went to each child's room. Kneeling beside their beds, I recommitted their lives and mine into God's hands.

I also prayed for forbearance. It would have been easy to blame my driving error on the weariness that comes from mothering conflicting personalities. But I couldn't. Grace is learned in weathering conflicts, as we'll see in the next chapter.

Something to Build On

1. The apostle Paul named the hardships he endured in ministry as his credentials. Read 2 Corinthians 6:3-10, paying special attention to the virtues of verses 6 and 7. Why would he list these with adversities?

2. What plumbline (standard of measure) for suffering did Paul drop in Romans 8:18-19? To what should we compare our present sufferings?

3. C. S. Lewis wrote, "God whispers to us in our pleasure, speaks to us in our conscience, and shouts to us in our pain."[4] How has that been true in your life?

4. Read Isaiah 35:3-4. What promise is bound up in the repeated phrase "will come"? How might this help us to "be still" before God?

Be still before the Lord and wait patiently for him.—Psalm 37:7a

Make sure that nobody pays back wrong for wrong, but always try to be kind to each other and to everyone else.—1 Thessalonians 5:15

4

If the Shoe Fits, Shine It

Bearing with Other People

The decor in our garage includes an old television cabinet, stripped of its tube and wires, with one shelf added to make storage for "outside shoes."

Crammed into that cabinet are several varieties of snow gear (from heavy-duty boots to old plastic moon boots), a couple pairs of knee-high rubber boots (for changing sprinklers), and several pairs of derelict tennis shoes (good for river-wading, painting, mowing lawns, and weeding).

When I clean the garage and stuff all those shoes and boots a little tighter, I sometimes think of paring the collection to one boot and one yard-shoe pair each. But that wouldn't cover all the bases for our lifestyle.

That motley collection is a good picture of people. One size, one style, does *not* fit all. Understanding this is crucial if we are to improve our interpersonal relationships.

I remember the afternoon my son came home from first grade with drawings of "What I Like" and "What I Don't Like." The positive side showed Legos®, our home, running, springtime and flowers, and his friends. But on the "not-like" side he drew the color black, war, locked doors on dark nights, and "my sister Inga."

My sister Inga? You can be sure I asked him about that! That paper prompted a mini-sermon about how God values each of us, as different as we are, and how we need to value each other. We're called to do that even when "valuing" demands seemingly impossible patience.

Forbearance—the Bible-time word for "people patience"—asks that we extend to others gracious tolerance of their shortcomings. It requires the ability to see beyond the quirks to the qualities of a person, beyond their thorns to the rose at the top of the stem.

The apostle Paul knew how tough this would be. He outlines the dimensions of forbearance in Romans 12:10-17:

■ Show real brotherly love to one another.

■ Honor others above yourself.

■ Be generous and hospitable.

■ Bless your persecutors.

■ Share others' joys and sorrows.

■ Live harmoniously.

■ Bury pride; associate with the lowly.

■ Avoid conceit.

■ Refuse to repay evil with evil.

If that isn't enough, Paul adds, "As far as it depends on you, live at peace with everyone" (v. 18). We have to take the initiative in loving troublesome people.

The problem is that people are . . . people. They're usually different from us. They don't do things in our approved fashion. They don't think the way they should (our way!). But God doesn't make people from just one cookie cutter. I think he enjoys his utterly infinite creation—"each one an original." And I believe he knew that the disparities between people would in the end be the most profitable to our development as well-rounded people.

"As iron sharpens iron," says Proverbs 27:17, "so one man sharpens another." When the sparks fly, we're apt to put keener edges on who we are. We're less satisfied with mediocrity and more inclined to mature intellectually, emotionally, and spiritually. As we learn forbearance, we learn better ways not only to bear with one another, but also to bear up one another.

> A man's wisdom gives him patience; it is to his glory to overlook an offense. *Proverbs 19:11*

Jesus improved on that by pinpointing the essential element of love. He said we're to love God with all our heart, soul, and mind. Then we're to love our neighbors as ourselves (Matt. 22:37-40). How do we do that? By going back to the dimensions of loving God and superimposing them on our relationships with others. When we love with our "minds," we love them through an intellectual under-standing; through "souls," with a spiritual perspective; with our "hearts," with emotional sensitivity.

Loving with Our Minds

Forbearance begins with personality, that complex bag of mannerisms and ways of living that makes each person an original. Nobody else has our fingerprints or our exact ar-rangement of personal traits. But our personalities do fall into certain groupings, just as those whorls at the ends of our fingers can be classified.

As many as 2,000 years ago Hippocrates recognized that people tend to express themselves in four different tempera-ments. He linked it to the imbalance of certain body "hu-mours" such as bile, phlegm, and blood, giving us the terms "melancholy," "choleric," "phlegmatic" and "sanguine."

His physiology hasn't been proven out by science. But his observations of behavior continue to provide insight into how to get along with others. Let's improve on Hippocrates' terms by relating people to shoes:

■ Tap dance shoes—enthusiastic, always talking

■ Walking shoes—creative, busy

■ Combat boots—driven, goal-oriented

■ Penny loafers—two paces slower than life

Somewhere or other, one of these personality "shoes" is going to step on your toes. We'll have to deal with people and their personality quirks all our lives.

Dancing shoes. Here come the Tap Dance Shoes. You can hear "Tappers" before you see them. They're talkers who come across as happy, vivacious, and friendly. But underneath that expressive facade are people seeking praise and affirmation. They may be insecure and easily swayed. Often they're disorganized and undisciplined. This characteristic frustrates people who prize dependability, accuracy, facts, and details. But Tappers want to save face and don't easily admit their problems.

If you want to make enemies with Tappers, point out their shortcomings. Paralyze them with guilt.

If you want them on your team, compliment them for their ability to get along with people. Share their joy. Support their dreams and hunches. Look for ways to help them achieve mutual goals.

Walking shoes. Many people, when they need to think, go for a walk or run. While their legs are occupied and extra blood is pumping through their cells, they deal with life.

Walking-shoe personalities are the thinkers, the creative introverts. They're sensitive to others, analytical, dependable, and meticulous. Their motto is, "If it's worth doing, it's worth doing right."

So what's wrong with that? First, because they're goal-oriented, they don't want to take risks or encounter surprises. They want a map of where they're walking. This annoys go-getters who want to jump into projects without getting dragged down over imagined problems.

"Walkers" also irk others with perfectionism, worry, doubt, and pessimism. They're prone to have a critical spirit and carry around a grudge list.

We need these people. Without them, more planes would crash, more cars would get recalled, and daily bureaucracies would be even more inefficient. We also need to be more forgiving when their impatience impairs their capacity to forgive.

They'll listen to advice. They might seem to reject it at first and brood. But they're thinking, and a gracious spirit will keep them on your side.

Walkers also tend to be diversified people who have developed many interests outside their profession. Their discipline makes them lifelong students. Tap into a pet topic and you'll affirm them as well as expand your own horizons.

Combat boots. Here's the driver temperament. "Boots" can alienate people as they pursue goals with tough, disciplined, determined power plays. They draw up to-do lists and forge through them like an army bent on victory.

You can't relax around Boots. But their dynamism is a necessary commodity. They do what the other personalities talk about, worry about, or avoid.

But Boots tend to be short-tempered, impatient, inflexible, and cold. They think others are trying their patience. In truth, they're trying others' patience! It's hard for them to admit they're wrong and apologize.

Boots need assurance of loyalty. They need people to pick up the details. They need junior salesmen. In other words, they need the support of the other personality types to achieve their dreams. And likewise, the others need the dynamism of Boots to keep them all going in one direction.

Penny loafers. "P-L" is the calm eye of the hurricane, a philosopher who pokes fun at the storm the other personality types create by their impatience with each other.

People are attracted to "P-L's" friendliness. He likes feeling safe, so he's usually easy going and enjoyable to be around. He's patient when provoked, a diplomat who seeks to help enemies hug.

But P-L also tends to be slow, unmotivated, and stubborn. He fears failure, so he'll hide his problems or simply not try.

A P-L needs to be surrounded by the other personality types for stimulation to set and pursue goals.

Getting a handle on these personalities has helped me in my family, church life, work relationships, and friendships. I tend toward the Walking Shoes personality—the detail-oriented, creative person prone to a critical spirit. One way that shows up is exasperation with people who are different, who don't think like I do! Giving them the freedom to express their God-given personality frees me up to love and accept them.

That's not to say, however, that we can arbitrarily categorize people and presume that we understand them. Each of us is a blend of these personalities, with one usually predominant. Sometimes I wear combat boots along with walking shoes—and what an awkward gait that is: demanding that people do things perfectly!

Nor should we use personality theory to excuse ourselves from change and balance. If we recognize our own laziness as a P-L, we need to link up with a Walker who can help us bring order and focus to our lives. Our goal is to become like Jesus, who balanced all those personalities in their positive aspects.

Loving with Our Spirits

Another aspect of "forbearance" is spiritual discernment where others are concerned. The spiritual reality is that people either have Christ living in them, or they don't.

> Therefore, if anyone is in Christ, he is a new creation; the old has gone, the new has come! *2 Corinthians 5:17*

When we're "in Christ" we have a new perspective, a new orientation, and a new ability to grow and change for the better. Those who haven't yet been reborn spiritually do not possess the same capacities. This basic spiritual difference is often the root of our conflict with others.

The book of Proverbs is quite blunt about the character of a person who is operating outside the power and influence of God's life. Our English translations rely primarily on the simple term "fool." But the three Hebrew words from which that word is translated paint in more detail the troublesome personality flaws that result from spiritual alienation.

Kesil (used nearly 50 times) denotes a person who is obstinate and falsely confident. He or she:

- likes to air his own opinions (18:2)

- cannot imagine himself mistaken (17:10)

- is apt to repeat his folly (26:11)

- won't face facts (14:8)

- despises God's wisdom (1:22)

- brings his parents sorrow (10:1), bitterness (17:25), and ruin (19:13)

- despises his parents (15:20)

Evil (used about 20 times) darkens the fool's reputation, carrying more a sense of stupidity and stubbornness. He or she:

■ spurns advice (1:7)

■ is convinced he has the answers (12:15) so chatters away rather than accepting advice (10:8)

■ spurns his father's concern and wisdom (15:5)

Nabal (used three times in Proverbs and resurfaces as the name of Abigail's impudent husband in 1 Samuel 25) adds boorishness. He or she:

■ has "arrogant lips" (17:7)

■ is grief to his father (17:21)

■ lacks any self-control (30:22)

Today's "fools" dismiss godly counsel. They marry out of God's will or live immorally. They're bound by addictions to drugs, drinking, gambling, living beyond their means, lying, and pursuing sensual pleasure. They're quitters who won't follow through on educational goals or ride out storms in the work place.

When I run into people like this, I recognize they're not only hampered by the negative aspects of their personalities but further impeded by an inability to change. Only Jesus Christ can change them from the inside out—and only when they're willing.

These interpersonal conflicts are a clear manifestation of spiritual warfare. God calls us to be kind, able to teach, and not resentful if we're spurned:

Those who oppose him he must gently instruct, in the hope that God would grant them repentance leading them to a knowledge of the truth, and that they will come to their senses and escape from the trap of the devil, who has taken them captive to do his will. *2 Timothy 2:25-26*

We may be the only "Jesus" others see. We may be the only person praying for them. Our friendship—our ability to become a part of their lives while still remaining strong in Christlike attributes—may be more important than we realize.

Loving with Our Hearts

People will also see Jesus in us when we show them what true forgiveness involves. Loving with our hearts means putting aside our grudge lists, our desire to take revenge, and our hurts. The Lord's Prayer says, "Forgive us our sins *as* we forgive those sin against us." Our ability to appreciate God's forgiveness of us is mirrored in our ability to offer forgiveness to others.

That's the point of the parable of the unmerciful servant (Matt. 18:21-35). Our Christianity will not become real to us until we convey to others the same mercy God has shown us.

Jane learned that the hard way through her relationship with Patty.

Jane (the perfectionist "Walking Shoe") met Patty (the free spirit "Dancing Shoe") at their singles Sunday school class. Soon after, Patty's world caved in. She had major surgery, lost her job, then lost her place to live.

Desperate, she called Jane and asked if she could move in for a few weeks until she got her feet on the ground.

Jane felt cornered. She cherished her privacy in a tiny one-bedroom apartment. But here was a Christian in need. How could she say no? So Patty moved in with all her plants and habits.

Soon their opposite personalities started clashing, complicated by extreme mood shifts related to Patty's illnesses.

Those "few weeks" became months of rent-free hospitality. Patty had a few job leads but felt that none was quite right.

Jane's generosity eroded to exasperation. She felt trapped. Their communication deteriorated.

One night Jane came home and found the apartment door open and the lights on. At first she feared a burglar until she stepped into the kitchen and found it strewn with dirty dishes. Her new plastic-coated cookie sheet bore half a pizza and fresh scars from an ambitious knife.

She found Patty next door, watching television. Jane seethed inside as she cleaned up, alone.

Then one night Jane came home to an empty apartment. Patty had abruptly moved in with someone else.

Jane thought her problems were over. But they weren't. Her anger over being "used" festered into an ugly grudge against Patty. They avoided each other. Jane found herself wishing ill upon Patty, unable to speak kindly of her.

But God got through to Jane. She began to see her hateful attitude as Jesus did, as murder (Matt. 5:21-22). It was right in there with "bitterness, rage and anger, brawling and slander, along with every form of malice" (Eph. 4:31). Genesis 50 especially troubled her. She saw how Joseph was able to forgive his brothers, even though they'd wronged him far more deeply than Patty had wronged Jane.

Jane knew she'd lost her joy and gentleness in the backwash of this soured relationship. For several years that corner of her life represented unfinished business. I know, for I was "Jane."

God showed me how clinging to that hurt was a prideful focus on myself and a refusal to acknowledge God's higher purposes. Maybe Patty's stay with me was the delay God needed to prepare her for her eventual job. More important, maybe I needed a "Patty" in my life to chip away at some spiritual calcification.

I was also wrong in waving the list of Patty's wrongs while ignoring my own pettiness and failure to communicate.

Once I confessed my sin to God, I knew what I had to do. Through friends I tracked down Patty's address and wrote her, asking her forgiveness for causing our rift.

I didn't expect a reply—"An offended brother is more unyielding than a fortified city" (Prov. 18:19). But a few weeks later she wrote, forgiving me and asking my forgiveness for her part.

Twenty years later, I still have that scarred-up cookie sheet. Thousands of cookies later, it looks terrible. But I keep it as a reminder of how forgiveness really works, of how important it is to learn to see people as God sees them.

We simply cannot afford to "trash" the people we cannot get along with. Jerry and Mary White, in *Friends and Friendship*, tell how Jesus led the way for us:

> Jesus showed an amazing tolerance for people of all backgrounds and peculiarities. When the religious leaders attempted to scorn him, they only revealed a strong point of Jesus' character by saying, "Here is . . . a friend of tax collectors and 'sinners' " (Matt. 11:19). It shocked the leaders that Jesus saw value in and claimed friendship with those who had chosen a life different from theirs.[1]

Jesus let others clop around in their combat boots, dancing shoes, walkers, or loafers. He could do that because he loved them totally and could see them for what they could be—in him.

He could also do that because he *was* perfect peace. His personality was balanced and fulfilled.

Our failure in relationships often comes down to that: failure within ourselves. God says to love our neighbor *as ourselves*. The next chapter will try to explain how that can happen.

Something to Build On

1. Which personality type probably describes you? Which one describes the person you have the most difficulty loving?

2. Check out the power of kind words in Proverbs 15:1, 25:15, and 31:26. Summarize the power in your own words.

3. Write your own proverb about revenge based on Romans 12:17-19, Ephesians 4:26-27, and 1 Thessalonians 5:15.

4. From James 3:17-18, list the qualities of peacemakers. Which traits are your strengths? Which need nurturing?

Be completely humble and gentle; be patient, bearing with one another in love.—Ephesians 4:2

You will keep in perfect peace him whose mind is steadfast, because he trusts in you.—Isaiah 26:3

5

That Gear Called Neutral

Achieving Inner Peace

We live in the McQuick era. We like to punch a button to close the garage door, then drive away to eat, bank, turn in film, get milk, buy medicine, pay bills, and dispatch dry cleaning with the ease and swiftness of an arm out the car window.

Forget parallel parking. Forget parking meters. Forget waiting and waiting to have your purchase rung up. Believe it or not, I saw a television special on a funeral home that offered drive-in casket "viewing"!

We're on the run, impatient with the pokiness of life.

I'm just as guilty as the next. One of my aggravating habits is jumping into conversations and finishing off what I thought the other person was struggling to say.

Do you see a man who speaks in haste? There is more hope for a fool than for him. *Proverbs 29:20*

Everyone should be quick to listen, slow to speak. *James 1:19*

True confessions time. Once I put kerosene in the lawn mower because I couldn't wait for my husband to come home and tell me which can had gasoline in it. Another time I was gung-ho to paint our bedroom. I didn't hold the lid down well enough when I shook the paint can, and "Ivory Linen" erupted all over a section of dark brown rug on my side of the bed. Despite frantic scrubbing, a haze remained. For two years, until we could afford new carpet, I looked at it and felt guilty.

A patient man has great understanding, but a quick-tempered man displays folly. *Proverbs 14:29*

For a long time I thought people who had tempers were just the ones who screamed, used naughty words, and threw things. But more and more I recognize that I have a temper problem that comes from a warped desire to conform the world to my agenda.

I waste a lot of energy warring at the lowest level of conflict, those "Murphyisms" (chapter 2) that irritate like rocks in shoes. But sometimes "Murphyisms" are my own doing, the result of a spirit that simply won't take "wait" or "no" for an answer. I've got my to-do list and I don't appreciate anybody reaching over and crumpling it up.

The apostle Peter knew just what I'm speaking of. When Jesus starting telling his disciples that he'd suffer and die, Peter wouldn't hear of it. Peter had other plans for Jesus and his kingdom. It reached a crisis in the Garden of Gethsemane when Peter sliced off the ear of the high priest's servant—as if that would keep Jesus from the cross! Yet years later, in mellowed insight, Peter wrote:

Make every effort to add to your faith . . . self-control, perseverance. 2 Peter 1:5-6

Peter had realized that walking with Christ meant adapting to Christ's pace—one that allowed for interruptions and yet accomplished his purposes.

The other option—and it doesn't succeed—is resisting life. It's like this poem that my children inspired:

Run in circles,
Scream and shout,
Blame the other,
Throw a pout.

Or, say this fast: "Put yourself in a pickle about phlegmatic, presumptuous, or petulant phonies or their piddling problems that pique us."

But as I tell my children, "Fussing doesn't get you what you want." We adults need that lesson, too. Fussing only reveals that we cannot accept the circumstance God has put us in. It is a symptom of an inner state of soul that has not come to rest with God, and therefore cannot live peacefully with others.

Achieving that peace takes work. It takes a deliberate effort to cooperate with God's Holy Spirit in bringing the negative aspects of our personalities under his guidance and fashioning. There are some general principles to help us through this process:

- Know your weaknesses.

- Respect the limits of time.

- Adapt to your circumstances.

- Accept your deficiencies.

Know Your Weaknesses

Intolerance is like chicken pox: highly contagious! We may need to be cautious about spending too much time with impatient people if impatience is our own weakness.

> Do not make friends with a hot-tempered man, do not associate with one easily angered, or you may learn his ways and get yourself ensnared. *Proverbs 22:24-25*

Rash people reinforce our tendencies to be rash. Negative thinking is like yeast, foaming through the dough faster than we realize. I've seen this replayed over and over during what's called "Arsenic Hour" at our home. That's the head-ache-hunger-hollering hour just before dinner. Two such stricken children in the same room tend to act like tom cats defending their territory. They're impatient with each other and with the world in general. We have to separate them, sending them to their rooms. Without one goading the other on, the battle ceases.

In the Big-People World, the same principle applies. I remember how lunch breaks brought out the gripes with a certain group. Over Thompson grapes we'd hear sour grapes; over baloney sandwiches we'd hear about working for peanuts. Sometimes I had to play the devil's advocate and suggest that the alternative to our jobs was no job, and despite the negatives we had a lot to be grateful for. Sometimes, knowing how easily I might be tempted to add to the complaints, I quietly found alternative seating.

Respect the Limits of Time

The impatient person wants a 25-hour day at the very least. There's never enough time for him to do all he wants—especially if he has the "walker" or "boots" personality. The remedy is to accept that there never will be enough time. He'll be frustrated until he drops some things from his agenda.

I'm stepping on my own toes here. Like the morning I got the beds made and dishes done, the first load in the washing machine, and both kids off to separate schools.

Then I scampered out to the car with barely two hours to make a bank deposit (drive-in, of course), drop off film for processing, pick up coupon items at one grocery, buy milk at a drive-in dairy, get stamps, leave used clothing at the thrift store, return library books (another blessed drive-in box), get knit ribbing for a sewing project, and buy the rest of the groceries at a warehouse store before arriving at my daughter's kindergarten for carpool duties.

Somebody must have greased the clock hands. By the time I got to the final store I was tempted to crash the "nine items only" line with my fifteen instead of waiting behind the lady piling two hundred dollars' worth of merchandise on a belt run by turtle power. Oh, no! She had 642 coupons and a dispute over the price of corn flakes. I was reduced to reading the latest tabloid scandal on Elvis's ghost and hoping that my little girl wouldn't cry because Mommy was late.

I'm all for the efficient use of time; I have a folder in my desk into which I tuck articles and ideas on time management. A lot of them help. But when, in my zeal for efficiency and productivity, I take on more than one life can hold, it shows in the way I treat others and in my body's stress signals.

But I am learning to plan out my commitments. I say "no" to a lot of good things when I sense that too much is stacking up. I may miss a great sale or an opportunity to serve on a committee. But ten years from now those things won't matter—certainly not as much as my being the kind of mother, wife, and fellow human being I'm meant to be.

Adapt to Your Circumstances

The Lord Jesus succeeded in accomplishing so much in three years because he flowed with his circumstances. In Matthew 9, for example, he was dealing with some criticism of his followers' lifestyle ("Why don't your disciples fast like the Pharisees?") when beckoned to town to raise a ruler's daughter from the dead. On the way a woman who'd given up on gynecologists tugged on his coat and was healed. He pushed through a crowd to raise the girl, then left and healed some blind men. Right after that some folks brought a demon-possessed man for healing.

Jesus didn't say, "Okay, all who need healing show up at 2 P.M. Those with demons I can fit in at 4:15. Raising the dead is heavy duty and a little more urgent. Be there promptly at noon." Instead, he allowed God to arrange the agenda. He worked and taught in an atmosphere of constant interruptions, yet he recognized that such is the case when people are needy, wandering "like sheep without a shepherd" (Matt. 9:36). In recognizing the nature of his ministry he was able to adjust and not get irritated when the day's plan went haywire.

Adapting to circumstances means being willing to put my schedule aside. That's hard for me. When my children took swimming and gymnastic lessons at the YMCA, we always had two bags: one for their clothes and one for Mom's projects. Ignoring the soaps on the lobby's television, I'd mend, knit, sort coupons, write letters, catch up on my magazine reading, or read a pocket-size New Testament.

There's nothing wrong with "redeeming the time." But sometimes time waits to redeem *us*. That became most apparent when we went fishing as a family. I had to leave my lists at the truck and launch out into discovering the "now." My children mirrored my tendency to fume when the first troll around the lake didn't do a bit of good. Within the first hour I could count on a few "I wanna-go-homes" and persistent requests for the snack bag.

But we were there to fish and to enjoy the setting. And so I'd point out the bugs flitting across the water or the concentric circles where a fish jumped. Our imaginations transformed clouds into bunnies and race cars.

Appreciating the "now" can liberate us from being discouraged or frustrated by circumstances. It frees us to thank God for what we see and who he is. Life in neutral can become a lot more peaceful.

Accept Your Deficiencies

Inner peace may elude us if we cannot accept being second-best. If we're always churning to be number one, to be recognized, we cannot accept God's plan for our lives.

One afternoon my son handed me a letter as he got out of his first grade classroom: "Dear Mom, I cryd in P.E. today becuse I dident win a game in P.E. Evreyon got me. Love Zach. P.S. I love Mom."

My son is a high achiever. He excels in detail work. You should see what he can do with a box of Legos®. His drawings are loaded with minutiae the size of a thumb tack. To be less than best bothers him.

There's another word for this problem: perfectionism. Perfectionists are people who live within the jails of their own impossibly high standards. They don't give themselves permission to be imperfect and are quick to put themselves down. Their rally cry is Matthew 5:48: "Be perfect, therefore, as your heavenly Father is perfect."

This verse comes out of a passage that urges Christ's followers to love even their enemies. This was radical teaching! When Jesus said, "Be perfect," he meant that we should strive to live as mirrors of God's perfect grace and generosity toward others, and, for that matter, toward ourselves. God knows we're scratched mirrors. No one is flawless and above making mistakes. We're *not* now perfect as God is perfect. But God is realistic about the process of spiritual growth. We need a goal: the perfection he *is*. Over the years, as he reconstructs our character, we come closer to that ideal. And we realize that we're just frauds if we pretend to be perfect now.

Achieving inner peace involves transforming the starchy demands of perfectionism into its kinder cousin, the pursuit of excellence. In his book *Measuring Up,* Kevin Leman, deals with this difference:

> The perfectionist reaches for impossible goals, whereas the pursuer of excellence enjoys meeting high standards that are within his reach.
>
> The perfectionist bases his values of himself upon his accomplishments, while the person who pursues excellence values himself simply for who he is.
>
> The perfectionist tends to remember his past mistakes and dwell on them. He is convinced that everyone else remembers them, too. The pursuer of excellence, on the

other hand, will correct his mistakes, learn the lessons they have to offer, and then forget about them.[1]

I get to apply the distinction between perfectionism and excellence whenever I play my violin or the piano in public. Sometimes I suffer a relapse of a childhood malady called Acute Recital Trauma. That's when a performance turns your knees to jackhammers and your hands to slime.

One Sunday I was scheduled for the piano offertory for the evening service. I'd diligently practiced the tricky parts, but when I sat down at that imposing grand piano, several hundred eyes watching, the Trauma hit. Smack in the middle I flubbed a note. Even though I recovered my run, it was obvious enough to my five-year-old (who'd heard the song over and over at home!); when I got back to my seat, she remarked in one of those child's whispers audible rows back, "You goofed, Mommy!"

Children are great for slicing perfectionists down to size! I could have brooded about how I destroyed the beauty of Fred Boch's "Clair de Lune" stylization of "Jesus Loves Me." But, trying to overcome perfectionism, I opted instead for believing that people caught a musical glimpse of God's love through the 90 percent of the piece I played right. I know God heard it as praise.

God is not in a hurry where our development is concerned. He's willing to hear wrong notes again; what he doesn't want is for us to give up and stop playing altogether, which is a constant temptation for the perfectionist.

God specializes in using blemished people. If I need proof of that, I can recite the names of people he chose to be the earthly ancestors of his Son. Luke's list includes a well-known adulterer and murderer, David. Matthew includes four women with splotches on their résumés. Tamar committed adultery with her father-in-law. Rahab was a harlot. Ruth had pagan roots. Then there was Bathsheba, whose rooftop bath instigated the sin eventually known around the world.

Yet our God is the God of grace. To think that in Hebrews 11 Rahab's faith was commended as an example to all of us! Like Rahab, we can know we are loved by God the Father. In spite of our imperfections and serious character flaws, in spite of our most hateful sin, we stand in the overwhelming light of Jesus' goodness—Jesus who was crucified and risen. We can say, "I am not perfect. But God sees me through the perfection of his Son, who came to make a way for me to be a true child of God."

We'll see a little more of how that love changes us—and challenges us—in the next chapter.

Something to Build On

1. Imagine yourself as Peter in those agonizing hours between his denial of Christ and the resurrection. What emotions do you think he would have felt? How did the empty tomb change all that? (See Acts 2:14-39.)

2. Read Psalm 34:17-19. What message does this passage offer to those who live in despair?

3. According to Isaiah 30:15, where does real inner strength come from?

4. Suppose Job asked you the question he raised in Job 6:11. What would you answer? Remember the commendation he later received in James 5:11.

He who began a good work in you will carry it on to completion until the day of Christ Jesus.—Philippians 1:6

Yet the Lord longs to be gracious to you; he rises to show you compassion. For the Lord is a God of justice. Blessed are all who wait for him!—Isaiah 30:18

6

When the Holy Meets the Lowly

Love That Endures for the Sake of Others

Perspective. It's what you need when life gets confusing, frustrating, or oppressive, like that messy garage.

Sometimes you just need to pull down the door and get away. Put yourself where you can get the big picture. Get close to God's handiwork.

Like the times our family goes upriver and into the little Entiat Valley, where a searching stream is splattered by the shadows of great trees and their offspring, where the forest floor is sprinkled with the colors that dropped off the Creator's paintbrush.

On one such hike I kept looking up at the splendor of Douglas firs, so tall that they seemed to almost snag the fleeced clouds racing overhead. The scene reminded me of God's might and power and unapproachable holiness. But a little tugging hand brought me back to earth.

"Pretty, Mommy, pretty!" insisted Inga, then four, as she pulled me down to look. She was captivated by a clump of daisies, pert white petals radiating from sunshiny velvet eyes. So fragile, so vulnerable, and yet so protected. I thought of Psalm 138:6: "Though the Lord is on high, he looks upon the lowly."

The high and holy. The sinful and lowly. The One who is lifted up in majesty and praise is also gentle and patient toward us.

Often we envision God as stern, unyielding, hard to please. But that's not so. A. W. Tozer observed:

> How good it would be if we could learn that God is easy to live with. He remembers our frame and knows that we are dust. He may sometimes chasten us, it is true, but even this He does with a smile, the proud tender smile of a Father who is bursting with pleasure over an imperfect but promising son who is coming every day to look more and more like the One whose child he is.
>
> Some of us are religiously jumpy and self-conscious because we know that God sees our every thought. We need not be. God is the sum of all patience and the essence of kindly good will. We please Him most, not by frantically trying to make ourselves good, but by throwing ourselves into His arms with all our imperfections, and believing that He understands everything and loves us still."[1]

We need to see this side of God. It helps us understand how and why we love the Lord our God with our total beings—our hearts, souls, and minds. It also lays the foundation for the second of the greatest commandments: to love our neighbors as ourselves (Matt. 22:37-39). We need a proper view of God, a heart broken like his, before we can turn and love the others he has created.

But we also need to understand—and worship—God's holiness. That's where I have special appreciation for the high liturgical tradition I experienced in childhood. Mondays through Saturdays my world was confined to the tight walls of tract housing. But Sunday! Reverently my father led the family to his favorite pew, five back on the left. Starchy in my Sunday dress, I watched as the solemnly robed choir paced down the aisle singing "Holy, holy, holy."

They filled the loft just off the chancel then paused before harmonizing a call to worship from Habakkuk 2:20: "The Lord is in his holy temple; let all the earth be silent before him."

I almost expected God to come out of the door where the pastor waited, or at least for his "cloud of glory" to sizzle over the altar area like it did in the tabernacle and temple of Old Testament days.

I've learned a little more since the days of those second-grade impressions! Now I know that our earthly costumes for holiness can hardly reflect a glimmer of God's glory. Even King Solomon admitted his magnificent temple couldn't contain God (1 Kings 8:27).

In our earth-bound blindness we need these feeble glimpses of the holy God:

The blessed and only Ruler, the King of kings and Lord of lords, who alone is immortal and who lives in unapproachable light, whom no one has seen or can see. To him be honor and might forever. Amen. *1 Timothy 6:15b-16*

How God's Mercy Is Different from Ours

God's essence is blazing purity. He could easily blast us from memory for our impurity. *Yet God has chosen to be a God of second chances*—a God who, without compromising his holiness, will bend to help us. He described himself this way to Moses:

> The Lord, the Lord, the compassionate and gracious God, slow to anger, abounding in love and faithfulness, maintaining love to thousands, and forgiving wickedness, rebellion and sin. *Exodus 34:6-7*

The word in Hebrew we translate "slow to anger" literally means "long of nostril"—that is, controlled in expressing anger. When my children's spats drive me up the wall, I find myself "long of nostril" when I take a deep, deep breath. Far more is God patient toward us. He endures our rebellion and rejection to demonstrate that the other side of his holiness is his mercy.

That principle was fleshed out for me the summer after I attended Bible school. Coming off a one-year crash course in Bible for college graduates, I felt I'd climbed several notches up the holiness ladder. (That's called spiritual pride!)

Then Meg entered my life.

I'd started a flunkey job with a book publisher, but I was so broke from college bills that I jumped at the chance to live rent-free as summer manager of the school's eight women's apartments.

Nothing fancy—furnished with metal bunks, ancient rugs, and worn furniture—the units were rented to any women in transition during the summer.

One was Meg. Beyond her tired jeans and bushy hair I saw a face too old for age twenty. And those eyes—right away I noticed how she avoided eye contact. Distrustful, I quietly advised her roommate not to leave money or valuables around.

A part of me didn't want to get involved in Meg's needs. My new editing job brought its share of stress and head-aches, and I didn't think I could handle more. Yet I sensed that Meg craved a friend.

She stopped by regularly. At first she wouldn't talk. She sat forlornly on the apartment's time-grayed green rug, her eyes like sad weights focused on snags and lint. I'd ask questions, trying to draw her out. But she'd stare in silence.

Finally, the ugliness of her past trickled out. Her voice soft and hesitant, she told of getting into drugs as a girl. She'd visited a motorcycle camp and drunk a soft drink laced with LSD. From there came wandering, witchcraft, sexual perversion, and a coat-hanger abortion.

My heart tightened like an angry fist as I listened. I grieved for this child-woman robbed of home and hope as she grew up. I relived her horrors in my own nightmares.

Meg said she'd become a Christian the previous year but hadn't grown much spiritually. She blamed her struggles in understanding Scripture on a brain pickled by drugs.

"Meg," I insisted, "Jesus can heal your mind and help you. He wants you to read your Bible. It's like cleansing water through your spirit."

Local churches were too cold and conventional for her. So I set up a Bible study with her and another girl. Meg came once. She'd done half her lesson but said her mind was too messed up to finish.

But she continued to visit me at odd times. I served her my favorite herb teas in my only china cup. I listened and tried to correct her garbled spiritual understanding.

I missed seeing her one week. I learned she'd gone to California to witness to old friends. When I asked her how it went, her eyes dropped to the floor.

"Did they offer you drugs?" I asked.

"Yes."

"Did you take them?"

"They put the needle right in my arm," she said. "I couldn't stop them."

Then there was a family friend in town, an older man who came for her Saturday afternoons for overnight visits with him and his wife.

Meg said she was scared of him because he tried to rape her. Believing her story, I pleaded with her to refuse to go with him. But she continued the visits. As I watched her get into his car, my insides churned. Was he truly wretched? Or was she lying?

Meg continued to play with our friendship. To build bridges, I typed a paper for her. I sewed her a dress. I left cookies.

In August the apartments closed for cleaning and our paths separated. I moved into a house with four other single women, and Meg caught a bus to roots several states away. But she kept in touch.

That first year she wrote frequently—long, confused, and sometimes angry letters. I dreaded seeing the envelopes bearing her scrawly handwriting. I knew they'd require sensitive and detailed answers.

She got mixed up with a pseudo-Christian cult. I despaired over how to counter its false teachings. I sent books on Christian basics such as Paul Little's *Know What You Believe* and *Know Why You Believe*.

I felt there was no progress. I starred verses in my Bible about fools who despised understanding. Surely that was Meg.

Finally I prayed, "Lord, I'm losing touch through long distance. And I'm just plain losing. Send some strong Christians to nurture her one-on-one."

By now my parents had died. Overwhelmed by grieving and legal responsibilities, I couldn't handle Meg's problems, too. Sometimes I simply didn't answer her letters for several months. When she persisted, even sending self-addressed, stamped envelopes, I prayed more earnestly for new Christian leadership in her life.

A few years later another letter came from Meg. I hesitated opening it, anticipating the same old problems. But God had heard my prayers for her spiritual nurture. Plus, she'd been accepted by a mission board as a printing technician and planned to go overseas.

The picture on her prayer card showed a renewed Meg. Her wild hair was shorter and stylish. Her eyes, though still too old, had softened. On the card were three verses:

I have considered my ways and have turned my steps to your statutes. *Psalm 119:59*

But seek first his kingdom and his righteousness, and all these things will be given to you as well. *Matthew 6:33*

For to me, to live is Christ. *Philippians 1:21*

A year later she wrote from language school overseas. Though unable to raise her full support, the mission had sent her ahead anyway to fill a critical office need. A few days later another letter came, from mission headquarters. Meg had been killed in an auto accident.

Stunned, I went to my desk and pulled out her prayer card. Tears came as the last part of Philippians 1:21 came to mind: "and to die is gain." Meg in heaven, cherished by God, had shed the scarred life for perfect life.

A few weeks after Meg's death I received a note from her coworker, whom I'd never met. She said she was sorry I hadn't known Meg years later when she had grown spiritually and made many changes. She said she felt privileged to watch many things unfold in Meg's life and that Meg had taught her more than could be put on paper. She added, "Wanted you to know that your life made a difference with her."

I felt one inch tall. I'd given up on Meg. But God hadn't.

As she responded to God, he was able to "make up for the years the locust had eaten" (Joel 2:25). The drug culture had ravaged her youth, but in Christ she became a new creation capable of leaving a spiritual legacy.

To think that this great lesson came to me *after* Bible college, after I'd sat under seasoned Bible scholars and learned a lot about God. But it took Meg to show me that knowing about God isn't the same as knowing God, and that being able to quote verses about God's enduring love isn't the same as being able to express that same love to those who flounder apart from him.

Redemption took on a deeper meaning for me. I'd passed Meg off as an "incorrigible" placed briefly in my spiritual foster care. But God saw her as his daughter, deserving sacrificial love. He looks at me the same way:

I was shown mercy so that in me, the worst of sinners, Christ Jesus might display his unlimited patience as an example for those who would believe on him and receive eternal life. *1 Timothy 1:16*

God doesn't wait for us to be humanly acceptable before we're divinely acceptable. We don't have to clean up the house before the cleaning lady comes. Bible teacher R. C. Sproul notes:

> If I had to wait for God to approve of everything I did before He could save me, I would still be a lost person. It is while we are still sinners that He loves us. That's a truth none of us dares forget.[2]

Jesus' Example of God's Patience Toward Us

God has valid reasons to be impatient with us. Christ showed us some of these reasons during his public ministry. He upheld the Father's holiness when he cleaned corruption out of the temple, blasted the pretentiousness of the Pharisees, refused to be a celestial magician, and dealt with the thick-minded, selfish demands of his disciples. But he also showed the Father's compassion for the weak and searching in the following ways.

He was patient toward forgetfulness. Case in point: the disciples, after feeding over five thousand people with five loaves and two fish. Afterward, they had picked up twelve baskets of leftovers. No doubt that "Wonderbread" was in their boat when a storm struck, threatening to swamp them. When Jesus came walking toward them on the water, they forgot he was a person of power. Not until he climbed in and the winds ceased did they again acknowledge him as the Son of God.

But history soon repeated itself. Another crowd of four thousand needed dinner. The disciples again worried about where to find enough food. Again, Jesus multiplied loaves and fish.

Are we any different? When tough times come, do we forget God's power and fret? My husband has one solution to spiritual forgetfulness. Inside the cover of his Bible he writes out his personal lists of times God met a difficult need. When trials threaten to overwhelm him, those lists help him remember that God is bigger than any difficulty.

He was patient in teaching others to forgive. Peter was trying to concoct a formula for forgiving people. He thought seven times was enough. But Christ turned the number to seventy times seven—in other words, beyond counting. In the parable of the Unmerciful Servant (Matt. 18:23-35) he underlined the teaching that God's grace doesn't hold grudges.

I had to deal with that lesson when a single friend found herself pregnant and abandoned. Though the premarital intimacy was a sin both man and woman shared, I hurt especially for the woman. I didn't even want to see or talk with the man. But the Lord turned my attitude around to see this person as he saw him, and to pray for him. I was convicted by something written by German pastor Dietrich Bonhoeffer before his execution by the Nazis:

> I can no longer condemn or hate a brother for whom I pray, no matter how much trouble he causes me. His face, that hitherto may have been strange and intolerable to me, is transformed in intercession into the

countenance of a brother for whom Christ died, the face of a forgiven sinner.[3]

Seeing that person through Christ's eyes helped me love the sinner, though not the sin.

He was patient toward ingratitude. Ten lepers came to Christ for healing. Ten went away gloriously healed. Only one, a Samaritan (hated "half-breed" to respectable Jews), turned back to thank Jesus for his healing. Christ was disappointed (see Luke 17:17-18), but he didn't demand their gratitude. He saw results beyond the immediate circumstance.

This is a good lesson for people involved in ministries of encouragement and service. A friend who helped her church's needy once admitted how weary she got of serving without thanks. Then one day she was struck by a some writings on Galatians 6:9-10—that those weary of waiting for Christ's return are often those weary of well-doing in Christ's absence. Putting the long-range view on her service provided motivation to continue.

He was patient with others' distorted self-images. Fiery Peter declared, "Even if I have to die with you, I will never disown you" (Matt. 26:35). A few hours later, fearing for his life, he denied any connection with Jesus. But after the resurrection, Peter emerged into a powerful leader of the New Testament church. Jesus looked beyond the disciple's bravado and failure to his potential.

I'm often guilty of judging people by how I once knew them. Yet I want people to know me for what I am now, not as what I was. How liberating to be loved without regard to past history!

71

He was patient with those looking for the truth. Nicodemus was steeped in religion, a Pharisee and member of the Jewish ruling council. But he was a seeker, even though he came to Christ at night out of fear for his reputation. When Nicodemus stumbled on the concept of being "born again," Christ didn't chastise him.

God's holiness demanded a commitment from Nicodemus, a confession of sin and admission that he needed God's new life within. But Jesus' patience and God's mercy allowed him to struggle and question. The Holy was patient with the lowly.

When I pray for modern Nicodemuses—my non-Christian friends and relatives—it's with ragged hope. Their "religion" is their job, car, health, or friends. Some may show up at church if it's convenient, but God doesn't fit into their way of thinking.

One time I sensed a wall between me and another person because of my persistent invitations to worship services and special events. Finally I said, "Please forgive me if I've been guilty of pushing. My heart's desire is not that you make up your mind about attending my church, but that you make up your mind about what you're doing with Jesus Christ."

"Oh, I'm a very religious person," my friend countered. "It's just that I'm very private about it."

Nicodemus would have said the same. But faith is not private. It's everything you are! When I despair over spiritual apathy, I'm brought back to the Lord's enduring love. He hasn't given up on people, and neither should I.

When the Holy is patient with the lowly, marvelous things can happen.

When the lowly waits on the Holy, he learns about the very heart of God. Noah will help us see that in the next chapter.

Something to Build On

1. Read Isaiah 48:9-11. What reasons does God give for showing forbearance?

2. The contrast of God's reaching out and our rejection of him is a repeated theme of Isaiah. With which verses in Isaiah 65:1-5 can you identify? Why?

3. In Nehemiah 9:29-31 how did God deal with the nation's arrogance? How might that apply to people today?

4. Read Isaiah 59:1. For whom could you pray the promise of that verse?

The Lord is not slow in keeping his promise, as some understand slowness. He is patient with you, not wanting anyone to perish, but everyone to come to repentance.—2 Peter 3:9

I am still confident of this: I will see the goodness of the Lord in the land of the living. Wait for the Lord; be strong and take heart and wait for the Lord.—Psalm 27:13-14

7

Wait-Watchers and Other Spiritual Diets

Enduring because of Eternity

Noah gets the prize for having the world's messiest garage. No matter that it floated. No matter that it held no cars. Heaping with muck, manure, and all manner of life, it became a sanctuary for fleshing out endurance.

Forget the sanitized, plasticized, trivialized arky-arky Noah of today's retellings. Noah met life's frustrations at their rawest. He sweat, smelled, got splinters in his thumb and straw up his nose. And in that condition, he faced God.

Noah's story didn't start with the animal parade up the gangplank. It began more than 120 years earlier when God gave him two assignments: Preach judgment and build a mega-boat.

No doubt there were days when holding on was tough. But endurance kept Noah sawing gopherwood by hand to frame a boat one and a half times the length of a football field. Endurance kept him declaring God's coming judgment to his laughing, unbelieving audience. Endurance kept him faithful until the last of the animals had been gathered.

Then endurance had its hardest test. The door to the ark was shut. And there, amidst the bleats, croaks, grunts, and whinnies of hundreds, perhaps thousands, of animals, Noah waited.

Seven days. Seven long, dry, stuffy days. Then the patter of rain drummed on the roof.

Endurance clung to God's promises as the floodwaters lifted the ark from its braces and thrust it into an oceanic battlefield. Endurance sustained Noah through forty days of incredible storms. Then endurance kept him focused for more than a year while the waters receded and he lived among the filth of caged-up animals and their offspring.

As Noah scratched off the days on the wall by his bed, I wouldn't doubt that he wondered how long he could endure. He never knew he'd someday be commended:

> **B**y faith Noah, when warned about things not yet seen, in holy fear built an ark to save his family. By his faith he condemned the world and became heir of the righteousness that comes by faith. *Hebrews 11:7*

Noah's endurance shaped him for sainthood. He learned to bear the unpredictable in raw faith that God would prove true to his promises. He endured what he thought was the limit of endurance, then found more asked of him. As Oswald Chambers wrote:

A saint's life is in the hands of God like a bow and arrow in the hands of an archer. God is aiming at something the saint cannot see, and He stretches and strains, and every now and again the saint says—"I cannot stretch any more." God does not heed. He goes on stretching till His purpose is in sight, then He lets fly.[1]

Endurance is a building block in the making of saints. Over and over God will ask us to wait and watch, then to wait and watch even more until we're nearly broken. He wants us to discard our self-sufficiency and embrace his all-sufficiency. The process may involve dealing with doubts, disappointment, despair, and even disease. But God wants us to hold on when holding on seems impossible. In his time, we'll emerge with renewed energy and stronger character.

Modern-Day Noah Lessons

My friend Marty, a librarian, is a positive, enthusiastic, educated single woman who loves God. Her Noah-lessons started in the late 1970s when she wound up five years of missionary service with Alaska Bible College. She'd not only gotten involved in the clerical work but also solicited and collected donations from the lower forty-eight states.

Mission accomplished, she moved to Illinois to live with a friend, Jinny, also a librarian. But her hope of matching her skills to a local library faded. Despite her credentials (a master's degree and nearly three decades' experience), she found herself in a frustrating assortment of part-time or soon-dissolved positions. None quite fit her (they included proof-reading and house-painting), but they put food on the table and kept the rain off her head.

When Jinny moved to a new job in Pennsylvania, Marty followed, hoping for better opportunities. But she found herself in a quandary called "overqualified." Not one to sit around, she thrust herself into any job possibility. She interviewed at an insurance firm, a lumber company, a tourist farm/greenhouse, a farm magazine, a military institute, and a college library. She answered an ad to clip newspaper articles for various magazines.

She tried working as an aide at a nursing home but couldn't handle the physical demands. Through a temporary help agency she obtained piecemeal work: running copy machines, typing address labels, helping a blind lawyer with his computer, and sending out tourist brochures.

For five weeks she worked in a greenhouse, debudding mums, filling pots, and transplanting tiny seedlings. Then came another eight weeks answering the phone for a cement construction company and typing contracts and bids.

This went on for twenty months. In the midst of it all, her father died.

These were Marty's "Noah months"—the time for trust despite the tedium and the trials. Noah had no time to sit and whine about his lot. He had to feed and water the animals, shovel the manure, gather eggs, milk cows, and probably exercise some of the beasts up and down the ark's cramped aisles. Even though he was a farmer by training, not a zookeeper, Noah patiently fulfilled the tasks put before him while he waited . . . and waited.

Imagine how Noah's heart jumped when the ark snagged on the mountains of Ararat. Imagine his disappointment when his feathered scouting crews (a raven and a dove) returned, unable to land on water. Imagine his elation when a second dove, seven days later, brought back an olive leaf, the first evidence of new life. How Noah must have shouted for joy! The waiting was nearly over.

Marty's "doves" were rumors of a possible library job in the next county over. There was one snag—the library's rule that its employees live in the same county. Marty and Jinny had already bought a house in a different county, closer to Jinny's work. Marty concluded that her residence disqualified her. But she did file her résumé with a seven-library federated system in a neighboring county. When someone else was hired, Marty wondered again why God was having her wait.

Then came a "dove" with an olive leaf in its beak. The woman who took that position had seen Marty's résumé, and recommended her to the librarian in the next county for a position opening in inter-library loan. The board decided to waive their rule that employees live in the same county—for that position only! Marty was hired. Her wait was over. She recalls:

> Through all that job-searching I sometimes felt like a second-class citizen. It was hard to live with so much uncertainty all those months. But I knew the Scriptures said God would never leave me nor forsake me. He was teaching me to be content whatever state I was in. When the job came, it was definitely miraculous, and it was definitely his doing.

Marty adds that Psalm 27:13-14 came repeatedly to her in those hard months of waiting: "I am still confident of this: I will see the goodness of the Lord in the land of the living. Wait for the Lord; be strong and take heart and wait for the Lord."

How Long, O Lord?

When God calls us to seasons of endurance, His promises about watching and waiting take on deeper personal significance. Those in the Psalms especially touch us because their chief composer, David, knew the agony of waiting for God to raise him to the throne while Saul's reign disintegrated.

When we haven't learned the grace of endurance, we're prone to demand, "How long?"

My soul is in anguish. How long, O Lord, how long?
Psalm 6:3

How long, O Lord? Will you forget me forever? How long will you hide your face from me? How long must I wrestle with my thoughts and every day have sorrow in my heart? How long will my enemy triumph over me?
Psalm 13:1-2

The answer to "how long" is "Long enough for God's wisdom." In his knowledge of all times and events and peoples, he has good reasons for delaying.

First, all the elements to fulfill the bigger plan may not yet be in motion. Maybe that plan includes other people and circumstances, each needing to come to a certain point of maturity or readiness.

Second, *we* may not be ready yet. We may be assaulting God with a demanding spirit—and maybe we couldn't handle the answer even if it were given to us. If God's word is no, we need the spiritual maturity to accept that and trust God's judgment. If his word is yes, then we need the spiritual maturity to accept the responsibility that comes with the answer—and to give God credit, rather than explaining success or fulfillment in terms of our own cleverness or achievement.

For many years I prayed "How long, Lord?" in regard to my desire for a husband. I knew backwards and forwards the Scriptures that say singleness is a gift. At age thirty-three, I wondered if remaining unmarried was indeed God's plan for my life, even though a part of my heart still quietly cried for a companion.

Perhaps losing both my parents when I was thirty-one increased my loneliness. Perhaps having once loved a man when I was in my mid-twenties kept that desire alive. But as I settled into a new state with a new job and a new church, I looked to God for new beginnings.

Then God arranged a phone call that turned my life upside-down.

A decade earlier I'd started my first job in Wenatchee, the orchard heart of Washington state. Fresh out of college as an English literature major, I wound up writing crime news, obituaries, and a recipe column for a small daily newspaper. If Noah thought he was an unsuitable zookeeper, he didn't have much on my job mismatch!

One of my coworkers and his wife invited me to their housewarming party. His wife had also deliberately invited Rich, a single young teacher from her school. They felt that Rich and I, both being Christians, might have something in common. I left the party interested!

Drawing on the emerging national interest in health, I later contacted him for an article on physical fitness. (After all, he taught physical education for kindergarten through sixth grade!) The article bloomed into a romance. But a year later he broke things off, deciding he wasn't ready for marriage. He wanted to clear school debts and finish required graduate work before taking on a wife.

I eventually left town with the "broken heart missionary call," and ended up assigned to mission headquarters in the jungles of Los Angeles. Two years there were followed by a year in Portland at Bible school and another year working for a book publisher while I saved money for graduate school.

I thought of Rich every so often. His mother sometimes sent a Christmas card, but she never mentioned him. I concluded he'd found somebody else and that God had other plans for me.

Then my parents died just as I started graduate school in Illinois. I moved home; it took nearly a year to settle their affairs. Then I resumed my studies, graduated, and was hired by a Christian magazine in Chicago. I signed my first book contract.

As I moved into a little apartment, it seemed that God had finally let me out of the "ark." Eight years of waiting, watching, and working—and I'd settled into what I assumed would be my new life. I got involved in music and discipleship ministries at church.

But God was working in ways I couldn't even imagine. The catalyst was an article I wrote for *Moody Magazine* about a love letter I'd written my dad just before he died. The piece mentioned how being hurt in a broken romance made it hard for me to relate to Dad as he grieved over Mom's death.

A friend back in Washington state read the article and knew at once the "romance" I'd mentioned was Rich. In fact, her sister-in-law was now dating Rich's cousin! By now, Rich had finished his education, cleared his school debts, and bought a home he was sharing with the cousin. One time he wistfully mentioned to the cousin that there was once a girl he should have married. The cousin told his girlfriend, who then told my friend.

I hadn't been in touch with my friend since leaving. But she knew I wrote our former pastor, now at a church across the state. Writing him, she wondered if Rich and I still might have an interest in one another.

Balking at playing matchmaker, my former pastor reluctantly wrote Rich, filling him in on my life and giving him my address and phone. My pastor emphasized in the letter that he did not intend to interfere or push.

So it was that one late winter day Rich called me in Chicago. I hadn't heard from him in eight years. When the phone rang, I thought it was another wrong number for a popular coed at a nearby university—I'd been getting plenty of those lately. As I realized who it was, I slid to the floor in shock. Rich asked permission to write.

As the weeks slipped by, my devotional times reminded me to *let God* be at work. In Ruth 3:18 I read, "Wait, my daughter, until you find out what happens. For the man will not rest until the matter is settled today." We settled it during my summer vacation and set a wedding date.

I'll never forget the amazement of the clerk when we went to the courthouse for our wedding license. She could not believe that here, at thirty-four and thirty-six, were two never-married people who got back together after eight years of silence.

Our years apart had changed us and mellowed us. We've had our adjustments (and still do). But it's become more and more apparent that God delayed our marriage because we needed more time in the ark. As a single, I had been better able to meet the disrupting challenges of my parents' deaths. I also know I had to learn to deal with a demanding spirit, especially the one that presumed God owed me a life partner. I had to accept that God would do things the right way, and at the right time.

I wouldn't have chosen the route I took to where I am now. I don't enjoy getting put on hold. But my time in the "ark" was God's way of working out a future far better than I could have arranged. Andrew Murray, 19th-century church leader and missionary statesman, said there is no better place for cultivating or displaying Christian patience than in waiting on God.

> There we discover how impatient we are, and what our impatience means. We confess at times that we are impatient with men and circumstances that hinder us, or with ourselves and our slow progress in the Christian life. If we truly set ourselves to wait upon God, we shall find that it is with Him we are impatient, because He does not at once, or as soon as we could wish, do our bidding. It is in waiting upon God that our eyes are opened to believe in His wise and sovereign will, and to see that the sooner and more completely we yield absolutely to it, the more surely His blessing can come to us.[2]

As Noah gazed on the purged earth and watched a rainbow of promise arch across the sky, he had evidence that God was true to his word. Months of misery in a noisy, stinky zoo had their purpose. Noah built an altar in the mud and worshipped. He had passed the course in endurance.

But there is more to character than the endurance that waits on God. Perseverance puts feet to the waiting.

Something to Build On

1. Read Psalm 130:5-6. Why do you think the last phrase is repeated? How must watchmen feel as night's blackness turns slowly to day? Has there been a "waiting place" in your life where you felt that way?

2. From Jeremiah 29:11, what "plans to prosper you" and "give you hope and a future" have involved waiting in your life? Or in someone else's life? What promise do verses 12-13 offer?

3. Second Corinthians 9:8 says "God is able to make all grace abound to you." A hymn related to the times we've exhausted our store of endurance is Hubert Mitchell's "He Giveth More Grace." Find it in a hymnal and sing it. Consider writing out the lyrics as a Bible bookmark.

4. Read all of Psalm 106, then go back to verses 13-15. Often in desert times we want to give up waiting for God's best. How could the Israelites' experience apply to you?

Surely this is our God; we trusted in him, and he saved us. This is the Lord, we trusted in him; let us rejoice and be glad in his salvation.—Isaiah 25:9

Therefore, since we are surrounded by such a great cloud of witnesses, let us throw off everything that hinders and the sin that so easily entangles, and let us run with perseverance the race marked out for us.—Hebrews 12:1

8

Beyond the Buttercup Race

Stretching to Persevere

You'll find my garden trowel somewhere on the left side of the garage. It's essential equipment for an annual spring race our children anticipate even more than the community's big 2K Fun Run for Kids. We're talking about the Zornes Family Buttercup Race.

For years my husband Rich and his mother have vied for the honor of finding the first buttercup of spring. So as soon as February's grays start hinting green, we head for a favorite hillside about twenty minutes' drive from home. Tramping through the mud, we search for the most promising bud.

Sometimes we've hit the hills too early and we have to return in a few days. But when we find that "candidate" just about ready to pop yellow, we scoop it into a margarine tub and smile all the way down the hill.

After a few days in a sunny window, it's usually ready for delivery to the loser's front porch with a quick peck at the doorbell and a run for anonymity.

If only real life were as easy as hunting buttercups. But often we're called to persevere—to keep on seeking God's will—when there are no possibilities visible.

Endurance asks us to hold up, to bear up, to withstand hardship without giving up. Perseverance asks the same, but it requires that we translate that steadfastness into a goal. It trains us to focus on God's purpose and then move toward it, determined to give it unremitting care despite opposition or discouragement.

One Greek word used in the New Testament for "perseverance" is *proskarteresis*. It designates constant, energized prayer in Ephesians 6:18: "Praying always with all prayer and supplication in the Spirit, and watching thereunto with all perseverance and supplication for all saints" (KJV).

Its verb form shows up in Romans 13:6, describing rulers "who give their full time to governing." In both cases, there is a sense of undistracted, focused work toward a goal.

That's also the picture given in Hebrews 12:1, of a runner so intent on his race that nothing but running to the finish line matters. But the Hebrews passage reminds us of four other principles of perseverance:

- Remember you're watched.

- Run light.

- Never give up.

- Keep your focus.

88

Remember You're Watched

"Therefore, since we are surrounded by such a great cloud of witnesses . . ."

The "therefore" refers to the roll call of the faithful saints in the previous chapter, Hebrews 11. Some think this means that saints in heaven are peering at our progress. But Scripture gives no explicit statement about whether those who have gone to glory are aware of what's happening in the world. Bible teacher Charles Pfeiffer remarks:

> God has not seen fit to reveal that detail concerning His children who have entered His presence. We are told, however, that they are with the Lord, they surround us like spectators in an arena, and their example of faithfulness in their respective generations should be an incentive to us to be faithful in ours.[1]

The important point is that we are on display as we run the race for Christ. Other saints are our example in training. But the "grandstands" may also hold those who, in this earthly life with us, are watching our diligence and focus, evaluating if Christianity really works. One woman told how watching her mother's faith persevere through her father's fatal illness gave her the encouragement to endure overwhelming problems in her own marriage. We may be unaware of times our lives demonstrate God's help. But we do know that our world wallows in hopelessness, and people give up all the time. They need to see that life in Christ offers a better, brighter perspective. God doesn't want "secret service" believers. He wants us to demonstrate that Christianity really works.

Run Light

"Let us throw off everything that hinders and the sin that so easily entangles."

The Moffat translation says, "We must strip off every handicap, strip off sin with its clinging folds."[2] Runners leave nothing to chance. Professional marathon runners may train at high-altitude camps to strengthen their lungs. They run with weights to strengthen their legs. But on the day of the race, they have stripped off everything but the essentials.

Similarly, we're to train to get ourselves in top spiritual shape. "Train yourself to be godly," Paul urged (1 Tim. 4:7). We're to shed anything that keeps us from doing God's best. Our impediments might be habits of excuse, procrastination, or compromise. We might be hampered by anger or anxiety. Such weights may seem impossible to untape, but they *can* come off as our relationship grows with Jesus. Other hindrances may be simpler to remedy. The word "no" and accountability pacts may help us deal with overloaded schedules that rob us of time with God and loved ones. An honest listing of priorities may show us whether leisure activities use up a disproportionate share of our emotional and mental energy.

Never Give Up

"And let us run with perseverance the race marked out for us."

There's no room to doubt our abilities or be haunted by past failures. The apostle Paul said: "Forgetting what is behind and straining toward what is ahead, I press on toward the goal" (Phil. 3:13-14).

Marathoners know they can't run the entire race with their throttles at 110 percent. To conserve their energy, they run with caution, keeping up a steady pace until the others fade, then easing into the lead. Their pace may vary, but they never stop running.

God works with us the same way. There will be slower times in our race, situations that make us wonder if the race has been called off. Eventually, all of us experience periods during which we feel we have learned nothing, accomplished nothing, and grown not at all. Sometimes growth is happening so deep within us that we can't perceive it at the time. But God says to persevere, to continue, trusting him to bring the finish line in sight. This perseverance spends time in God's presence when prayer seems impossible; it continues to associate with other members of God's family when none of them seem to understand or care enough. Perseverance keeps doing the things it knows it should be doing, even when there is no clear instruction for the next step.

Keep Your Focus

"Let us fix our eyes on Jesus, the author and perfecter of our faith, who for the joy set before him endured the cross, scorning its shame, and sat down at the right hand of the throne of God."

We're not running for ourselves. Down at the finish line is the One for whom we live. The One who died so that we could truly live. The One who made it possible for us to live forever. The One we worship. And it is because of Christ that we can share this life with those in that "great cloud of witnesses," both those who have passed on ahead of us and those walking with us.

That's why I read Christian biographies: to be reminded of the faith that perseveres. It's why I'm reading such books aloud to my children at night, so that they have input as they grow in Christ. It's why I'm grateful to have met some who surely qualify for that "great cloud," who live among us even today.

One is Harry Lee. Friends from my church met him during their seminary years together. His life so touched theirs that they brought him to our church to share his story.

Born into a well-to-do Chinese family, Harry had the advantage of a good education. But his father died when he was a boy. As the family's wealth evaporated, Harry, as the oldest son, was left responsible for his mother and siblings.

From his teenage years, Harry had loved and served the Lord. One May night in 1956 in Shanghai, following a secret centennial celebration of missionary Hudson Taylor's arrival in China, Harry yielded to God's call to full-time service. It was a dangerous decision, for pressures under the Communist government were escalating.

Yet Harry turned to Scripture and summarized his commitment with Hebrews 12:2: "looking unto Jesus."

As friends in China and other lands heard of his decision, they urged him to attend seminary. Accepted by one in Hong Kong, he shocked his superiors by resigning his job in a state-owned company and turning to full-time leadership in his church, while working his way through the red tape necessary to study abroad.

In the meantime, close friends left the country and established themselves in lands of freedom.

But Harry had his call from God, plus love for Nadia, a graceful, gentle young woman he had met at the Endeavourers Church in Shanghai.

As their relationship deepened, so did the violent oppression by Communism. Nadia's family got permission to leave for Australia, but Harry's requests to take seminary studies out of the country were repeatedly denied.

Finally came that last night together in 1959. As they talked in the silent, dark church sanctuary, he urged her to forget him. She said she wanted to wait for him.

Broken-hearted, Harry tried to remain firm. He'd been denied permission to leave China so many times he felt as if his legs were in a bear trap. He had nothing to promise her.

When she insisted that they wait for each other, he pledged to wait and pray for her. But, he urged, if she met someone else who was right, he wanted her to go ahead and marry.

"Then write me a letter," he said, "so I'll be free from this promise. Otherwise, as a Christian and a gentleman I'll keep this promise."

In 1961, the government closed Harry's church. Officials harassed his family; then one night Red Guards stormed his apartment and ripped open ceilings, walls, and floors seeking "evidence" that he was a conspirator against the government. Angry, relentless questioning attempted to get a "confession" from him.

As Harry held firm, he recalled that one of the fruits of the Spirit is patience, and that reminder put him at an advantage:

> I've learned patience at the feet of the Lord. These people can't understand patience. They're like tigers . . . they've got to be off . . . they can't wait. Even if they try to beat out of me what they want to hear, they will go eventually. . . . I can wait.[3]

He was ridiculed publicly for trumped-up charges and allowed to return to his home. Again and again he was denied permission to leave the country. His brother, whom he'd led to Christ, died on a prison farm.

Finally, ten years after his acceptance by the Hong Kong seminary, Harry joined a group attempting to escape China aboard a fishing junk. They planned to hide under a load of fish as the boat crept in darkness out to freedom. He never made it aboard. He was arrested and spent ten months in a filthy, overcrowded prison.

On Christmas eve, 1968, he and other prisoners were trucked, hand-cuffed, to Shanghai City Stadium. Harry had been there before for badminton and volleyball matches; now it was an arena for public sentencing.

His turn came: "The prisoner venomously attacked the various political movements of the great Communist Party in his church services. Further, he betrayed the state and tried to desert to the enemy by seeking to escape. Seven years . . ."[4]

Harry was shipped to another overcrowded prison for seven years of deprivation and harassment. His days passed in a cell so narrow he could touch both its sides at the same time. Designed for one, it held four men and was so crowded that at night they couldn't sleep four abreast. Instead they alternated—the feet of one at the head of another.

Hunger haunted constantly and drove them to eating toothpaste and skin ointment. They supplemented their diets with egg shells and poured water into their rice to create an illusion of fullness.

Brainwashing and torture filled days and nights. Other prisoners, deciding they could take it no longer, committed suicide. Harry found comfort, strength, and guidance in the

"Bible" he'd smuggled into prison—not one of paper but portions of God's Word he'd memorized.

Torture was vicious. One time, hoping to get a confession out of him, officials manacled his upper arms so tightly that Harry nearly passed out in pain. The iron claws sliced into his flesh so cruelly that Harry feared he'd lose his arms from protracted lack of circulation. He kept his arms, but scars of broken skin remained.

When his term ended, officials decided he hadn't been brainwashed enough, so sentenced him to another four years at a prison farm. His health broken, Harry thought he'd die there.

During that time, China began to change. Mao Tse-Tung died. The U.S. and China edged toward renewed diplomatic relations. In 1979 Harry was released to tend to his mother, who was gravely ill.

Friends urged him to appeal his case, but that meant persevering through a convoluted bureaucracy. Finally one day he stood in a courtroom with several others and was pronounced fully exonerated, innocent of all charges. He'd spent eleven nightmare years in prison. His name cleared, once again could he work, shop, and travel.

When Harry first yielded to God's call to the ministry when he was thirty, he looked forward to forty years of service. Now he was fifty-four, his health scarred, his remaining years few. Yet he determined to try again for permission to study in a seminary abroad.

Twenty-six times his application to leave was denied. But God was at work, expediting that passport as well as preparing a place in a U.S. seminary. The twenty-seventh time he walked away with that precious passport in hand. It had taken *twenty years*.

That's perseverance.

In 1981, at age fifty-six, Harry boarded a plane for the United States and, as the first theological student permitted to leave China, enrolled at Western Evangelical Seminary in Portland, Oregon.

But that's not the end of his story.

He never forgot Nadia. For twenty-two years he had prayed for her. After his release from prison, he learned that a rumor had spread that he had died there. Nadia, who'd since moved from Australia to British Columbia, was married to someone else and had a five-year-old son.

Harry was stunned. "Lord, he pleaded, "You answered my twenty-four-year prayer to leave China to study in a seminary. Why wasn't my twenty-two-year prayer for Nadia answered the same way? You gave her away to another man!"

Then Harry thought of the apostle Paul, who carried on his ministry unmarried. "If you want me to do your work like Paul," Harry added, "I'll say amen. I'll sing a solo if you want me to sing a solo, I'll sing a duet if you want me to sing a duet."

During Harry's second year at seminary in Portland, Oregon, Nadia's husband was killed in a car wreck. Harry called and expressed his sympathies. But he held no hopes and didn't want to raise any for her. His heart was set on returning to China as a pastor.

But God's hand was at work. As Harry graduated from seminary in 1984, he was granted political asylum in the United States and became a mission representative-at-large with OMS, whose missionaries had long ago influenced his life for Christ. His new role meant travel around the world to tell of his experiences and the grace of the Lord Jesus.

In the fall of 1987 a speaking invitation took him to a church in Vernon, British Columbia, half of whose members remembered him from Shanghai thirty years before. In the third row, flanked by her mother and son, sat Nadia.

My goodness, Harry thought, *that's the girl I fell in love with thirty years ago. She's got a few crow's feet around her eyes now, but she looks just as beautiful to me as she did those many years ago.*

They didn't have much chance to speak to each other because Harry was whisked off to another church meeting. But the following August, on his first vacation since coming to the United States to study, Harry went up to see Nadia for two weeks.

They discovered their pledge to wait for each other was altered by two forgotten letters. Harry once wrote her a letter which essentially said:

> Forget it. We're not being realistic. I've applied to leave for so many years. It's hopeless. They're not going to let me out. I've lost my job and on top of it I have tuberculosis. I don't think I'll recover so forget about us. I want to release you.

But the persecutions of prison—beatings, sickness, and suffering—had dulled his memory about sending that letter.

Nadia, on the other hand, had forgotten to write the promised letter telling Harry that she had married. Not knowing this, Harry had continued to pray for her daily, remembering how that last night together in church in China he'd quoted her Romans 8:28, about all things working together for good for those who love God. Harry had interpreted that as believing God would unite them some day if they were his choice for one another.

Their two weeks together helped bridge more than two decades apart. On December 21, 1988, at the age of 63, Harry

Lee married the sweetheart of his youth. They chose the 21st of the month, Harry said, "for a twenty-one-gun salute to the One who brought us together in the first place, and then brought us back together again thirty years later."

Against all odds, but within the embrace of God's loving will, Harry came to know the full joy from persevering in Christ.

But running the race is only half the story. At the finish line it's another world. And our impatience for someday seeing that world fuels our capacities for spiritual perseverance.

The next chapter focuses on the goal toward which the many aspects of patience—longsuffering, forbearance, endurance, and perseverance—all aim.

Something to Build On

1. Read James 1:2-4. What does the testing of our faith develop? What is the finished work of perseverance?

2. A favorite hymn in one mission organization was this: "Faith, mighty faith, the promises, that looks to God alone/Laughs at impossibilities and shouts, it shall be done!" What scripture comes to mind from this hymn? (If none come to mind, check Hebrews 11:6 for one.)

3. Read Hebrews 10:36-39. What is "promised"?

4. What personal inspiration can you take from Harry Lee's testimony? How is 1 Corinthians 4:11-13 descriptive of his quest to serve God?

Therefore, since we are surrounded by such a great cloud of witnesses, let us throw off everything that hinders and the sin that so easily entangles, and let us run with perseverance the race marked out for us.—Hebrews 12:1

Run in such a way as to get the prize. Everyone who competes in the games goes into strict training. They do it to get a crown that will not last; but we do it to get a crown that will last forever.
—*1 Corinthians 9:24b-25*

9

Crowns from Crucibles

Persevering to the Prize

Say "crown" and many envision the magnificent British Imperial State Crown, refashioned for Queen Elizabeth II in 1953. It's crafted from three pounds of gold and well over 3,000 diamonds, sapphires, emeralds, rubies, and pearls. Its most famous gems include a flawless 317.4 carat diamond (cut from the largest diamond ever found, weighing one and a half pounds), the "Black Prince's Ruby" (the size of a small hen's egg), and a 104-carat blue sapphire.

Crowns weren't as elaborate in New Testament times. The Greek word for crown, *stephanos*, meant something that encircles. Winning athletes and others who were honored publicly were given garlands of oak, ivy, parsley, myrtle, or olive, leaves, or gold imitations of these. First Corinthians 9:25 even speaks of runners getting "a crown that will not last." But history's greatest crown was also its most primitive:

> They stripped him and put a scarlet robe on him, and then twisted together a crown of thorns and set it on his head. They put a staff in his right hand and knelt in front of him and mocked him. "Hail, king of the Jews!" they said. *Matthew 27:28-29*

We too easily run over these verses when following Jesus' journey to the cross. We shouldn't. Our Lord's crown of thorns holds great significance.

Here he was, King of the Universe, worthy of a crown exceeding even the world's most magnificent crown. But he allowed his spiritual monarchy to be mocked by a crown of thorns.

Why thorns? They resulted from the curse on the ground after humanity's fall in the Garden of Eden (Gen. 3:18). Jesus wore them as "King of the Curse":

> Christ redeemed us from the curse of the law by becoming a curse for us, for it is written: "Cursed is everyone who is hung on a tree." *Galatians 3:13*

Jesus' crown was most likely woven of the thorns which abound in Palestine. Stems produced thorns sometimes two inches long and pin-sharp.

The soldiers who crowned Jesus had already mutilated his back with a whip braided with bones and pieces of metal. When they jammed the thorns on his head, profuse bleeding from scalp wounds compounded his pain and disfigurement. This is the hurting, injured Jesus of whom Isaiah prophesied: "His appearance was so disfigured beyond that of any man and his form marred beyond human likeness" (Isa. 52:14).

Stop and think about that.

William Featherston (1846–1873) did. He wrote, "I love Thee for wearing the thorns on thy brow; If ever I loved Thee, My Jesus, 'tis now." That hymn expresses my heart when I consider the irony of crowns.

It is a great mystery—*God's Son should endure thorns, that we may wear crowns that last forever.* When we have run the race—when the Father is done remaking us into complete and truly holy people—we will go to the victor's stand and accept the crowns of heaven.

Scripture tells us of four different crowns prepared for believers:

- The crown of righteousness

- The crown of life

- The crown of rejoicing

- The crown of glory

The Crown of Righteousness

This crown is for believers who look forward to Christ's return. Paul described it in a letter near the end of his life, when he felt just about emptied out. "For I am already being poured out like a drink offering, and the time has come for my departure" (2 Tim. 4:6).

This is the man who endured the catalog of persecution and hardship. Second Corinthians reveals imprisonments, floggings, lashings, whippings, stonings, shipwrecks, and danger from bandits and enraged countrymen. He knew sleeplessness, hunger and thirst, cold, nakedness, plus the pressures and concerns of new churches and new believers.

But, he added, he wouldn't boast about these afflictions. When old soldiers get together, they talk about their battles and show off their medals. Not Paul. He'd rather boast about his weaknesses and how God could use him in spite of himself. This same man came to the end of his life and declared:

> I have fought the good fight, I have finished the race, I have kept the faith. Now there is in store for me the crown of righteousness, which the Lord, the righteous Judge, will award to me on that day—and not only to me, but also to all who have longed for his appearing.
> *2 Timothy 4:7-8*

Paul's "crown of righteousness" was an emblem of the changes God's spirit had brought about in his life. Granted by a righteous Judge, this crown goes to those who yearn to see the Lord Jesus and won't be ashamed to face him.

It's the crown for those who are so full of gratitude for salvation that they cannot contain their praise for God's amazing grace. "No condemnation now I dread," exulted hymn writer Charles Wesley (1707–1788). "Jesus, and all in Him is mine!" I can imagine him singing through tears—because I do!—the rest of that verse from "And Can It Be":

Alive in Him, my living Head,
And clothed in righteousness divine.
Bold I approach the eternal throne,
And claim the crown, through Christ my own.
Amazing love! How can it be
That thou, my God, shouldst die for me!

The Crown of Life

This crown is the reward for those who allow the love of God to reign in their hearts and sustain them. It's cast in the crucible of trials, which refine our character:

> Blessed is the man who perseveres under trial, because when he has stood the test, he will receive the crown of life that God has promised to those who love him. *James 1:12*

> Be faithful, even to the point of death, and I will give you the crown of life. *Revelation 2:10*

This crown takes the tears, prayers, and pain of persevering faith and transmutes them into a glorious prize. Bible teacher Harold Fickett adds this perspective:

> In the ancient world, the crown signified at least four things. . . . joy, royalty, victory and honor. These four concepts tell the story of the patient Christian's eternal reward. Because of his faith in Christ, he will win the victory over sin and death. He will be ushered into the presence of the Lord where as royalty he will share in the eternal inheritance of the King of kings. He will be elevated to a

place of honor. All of this will result in his experiencing unspeakable, indescribable, everlasting joy.[1]

The Crown of Rejoicing

This is the first of two crowns related to kingdom work. The apostle Paul's "crown of rejoicing" was comprised of people he'd won to the Lord. They were his trophies of grace.

> For what is our hope, our joy, or the crown in which we will glory in the presence of our Lord Jesus when he comes? Is it not you? *1 Thessalonians 2:19*

> Therefore, my brothers, you whom I love and long for, my joy and my crown, that is how you should stand firm in the Lord, dear friends. *Philippians 4:1*

I believe my great-grandmother Rachel Neely wears this crown. Though we had only limited contact when I was a child, I'll never forget seeing her sitting in my dad's upholstered rocker, alternately reading her Bible, crocheting, and closing her eyes to pray.

One time I asked her to sign my little red autograph book. Already my friends had inscribed such gems as, "When you get old and think you're sweet, take off your shoes and smell your feet." I thought Great-Grandma, with more than seven decades of knowledge, could surely top that.

Instead of a silly ditty, she wrote a Bible verse as an autograph for my life: "I have no greater joy than to hear that my children walk in truth (3 John 4, KJV)."

Great-Grandma had her sights on spiritual rewards. In her later years she prayed and fasted a day a week for her family. Finally, strokes moved her within inches of eternity. From her bed in a nursing home, she wept as she recalled a vision of heaven: "I was on the Glory Road and Jesus wanted me Home." A few weeks later she was there.

Forty years later, those prayers for her descendants have borne fruit. Her crown of rejoicing must be full of gems!

The Crown of Glory

Faithful pastors are candidates for this crown: "And when the Chief Shepherd appears, you will receive the crown of glory that will never fade away" (1 Peter 5:4).

The context admonishes pastors to care willingly for the flock of God, out of love, not greed and pride. As shepherds they are to abstain from seeking glory in their ministry. As their reward they will share in glory.

We need to be reminded about this crown when tempted to set spiritual leaders apart as unapproachable super-stars. As a writer and speaker, I know how easily pride and position can entrap. At one retreat where I spoke, a woman remarked, "I appreciate how you sit at meals to talk with us ordinary people. Usually the speakers just sit with the leaders." I assured her I was quite ordinary myself! I remember that Jesus said the greatest in his kingdom is the one who serves, not the one who expects to be served.

In Romans 16, Paul gave us a starter list of those deserving this crown, listing those who worked extra hard in the Lord. Some, like Apelles, were given extra commendation as those "tested and approved" (Rom. 16:10). As martyred missionary

Jim Elliot used to say (referring to 2 Timothy 2:15), it's the degree of "A.U.G."—"Approved Unto God."

God's Word also suggests what we should do with these crowns.

First, we're to guard them. Jesus warned: "I am coming soon. Hold on to what you have, so that no one will take your crown" (Rev. 3:11). We need to guard against false teaching that distorts the simple truth of salvation into a complex system of do's and don't's. We need to be wary of those who pervert the anticipation of Christ's return into elaborate speculations. Jesus said that he's coming soon, and that is all we need to know.

Second, we're to give them back to God. On earth, crowns are used for personal honor; but this is not the case in God's kingdom. In Revelation 4 we see through John's vision the throne of heaven, surrounded by the twenty-four elders' thrones. Dressed in white and crowned with gold, the elders remove their crowns and lay them before the Creator, declaring:

> You are worthy, our Lord and God, to receive glory and honor and power, for you created all things, and by your will they were created and have their being. *Revelation 4:11*

What a picture of unbridled worship we see, as those who are crowned willingly give back the symbols of their heavenly authority and rewards! Their adoration has been interpreted by great hymns of the church:

> Holy, holy, holy! all the saints adore Thee,
> Casting down their golden crowns
>   around the glassy sea. . . .
> —"Holy, Holy, Holy" by Reginald Heber

Changed from glory into glory,
'Til in heav'n we take our place,
'Til we cast our crowns before Thee,
Lost in wonder, love, and praise!
—"Love Divine" by Charles Wesley

Envision it: simple people, famous people, people who served Christ all their lives, people who came to him later in life. Crowns by the millions, all heaped in adoration before God. The concept is so wonderful, so incredible, that sometimes even our greatest hymns seem so feeble to describe it:

Crown Him with many crowns,
The Lamb upon His throne:
Hark! how the heav'nly anthem drowns
All music but its own!
—"Crown Him with Many Crowns" by Matthew Bridges

All hail the pow'r of Jesus' name!
Let angels prostrate fall,
Bring forth the royal diadem
And crown Him Lord of all!
—"All Hail the Power of Jesus' Name" by Edward Perronet and John Rippon

We're in process for those crowns all our lives. But our years against the length of eternity are brief, very brief. Sometimes we think our lessons in patience have gone on too long. We've endured to the utter edge of endurance. We've allowed for others' shortcomings until our faith in people has nearly eroded. We've waited and waited for God to act.

But against the immensity of God's time, our preparation for sainthood is infinitesimal. Our years are shorter than the hyphen between each hymn writers's birth and death date.

Eternity is near, very near. And with the end will come the songs of triumph.

When we get to heaven, we'll realize that crowns are only part of the expectation.

> To Him shall endless prayer be made,
> And endless praises crown His head;
> His name like sweet perfume shall rise
> With every morning sacrifice.
> —"Jesus Shall Reign Where'ere the Sun" by Isaac Watts

In the next chapter, we'll squint into a tiny crack of that wall between heaven and earth.

Something to Build On

1. Look at Daniel 12:3. What "crown" could this verse refer to?

2. A primitive goldsmith knew his gold was refined when he could see his face in it. When God refines us, he'll know we're ready for crowns when he sees his reflection in us. What further insight about refinement do you get from 1 Peter 1:6-7?

3. What might you sign in an autograph book? What would it reflect about you?

4. Which hymn portion was most meaningful to you? Why?

Blessings crown the head of the righteous.—Proverbs 10:6

I know that my Redeemer lives, and that in the end he will stand upon the earth. And after my skin has been destroyed, yet in my flesh I will see God.—Job 19:25-26

10

Worth It All

Living in Hope

Heaven must laugh at garage sales.

We are so absorbed in getting stuff, and then we turn around and re-sell it, or our descendants have to! There are no U-Hauls behind hearses.

Often we're like my children when our family gets ready for an annual garage sale. They pick over their piles of fast-food "happy prizes," which brought about five minutes of so-called "happiness." A few months later, these trinkets languish in the 25-cent box!

Toward the end of garage sale days, when I sit alone by the cash box, I sometimes gaze at the sky and wonder what it will really be like when we give up our trinkets forever.

I remember my impressions when I toured the Billy Graham Center Museum on the Wheaton College campus in Illinois. One special exhibit, "A Walk Through the Gospel," ended in a chamber of mirrors. I felt like I was floating in clouds, far, far away from earth.

As a sound system filled the room with Bach's B Minor Mass, I stood at the exhibit railing, letting my spirit soar, recalling Revelation 5:12: "Worthy is the Lamb, who was slain, to receive power and wealth and wisdom and strength and honor and glory and praise!" Tears came as I yearned to see the Lamb of God and to be caught up in adoration. Then others came through the exhibit, chatting and laughing, bringing me back to earth.

Heaven is the consummation of all patience. It's God's indescribable delight for his children. It's his blazing, loving, holy presence. It's something for which we just can't find words, except for what we've been told by the One who came from there, Jesus Christ.

As mortals we know how to describe and recommend travel destinations. My husband and I celebrated our tenth wedding anniversary with a trip to Kauai, Hawaii. (It was a vacation during which we learned patience because the children and Murphy's Law accompanied us!) So when a friend bubbled that her husband was taking her to Kauai for their tenth anniversary, I was full of advice on everything from beaches best for snorkeling to fresh produce at the local farmer's market.

But I can't speak as authoritatively of heaven. I only know what the Bible preserved of Jesus' words. He was confined to earth's vocabulary and concepts to describe his eternal dwelling place. What we know is wonderful. But God is asking us to trust him that it's even better than that. He has let us see just enough of the finish line to help us persevere for the prize.

Jessica, 10-year-old daugther of my friend Dianna, was diagnosed with terminal cancer. "Mom, are you going to

114

miss me?" Jessica asked one day. "Of course I'll miss you," Dianna replied. "I won't miss you," Jessica added, to her mother's surprise. "The Lord says a thousand years are but a day with him." What a grasp of eternity from one who died just days before turning 14!

"Forever" and "eternity" are difficult concepts. Yet we know heaven's "forever" is as certain for those who follow Christ as hell's "forever" is certain for those who reject him. There is no middle ground.

Heaven's "forever" will be the great equalizer, bringing together people from every nation and tribe. No matter what our color or language, God sees us in love as people under construction. He's alongside as we work through each day's disappointments and challenges. He asks us to trust in the wisdom of his master blueprints because he knows how fantastic the final results will be.

The Journey of Joy

Eternal life and the glories of heaven are not the only incentives we have for growing in godly character. The many facets of patience we have explored shape our lives here and now.

Bernie May, an executive with Wycliffe Bible Translators, saw this a few years ago while attending dedication celebrations for the Manobo New Testament, translated for people on the southern Philippine island of Mindanao.

As he traveled to the Manobo village, he was struck by their poverty. Eight people slept in an unwalled, thatched-roof hut with a split bamboo floor. Inside were a kettle, a knife, and some ragged clothes. But as 200 people gathered to worship on crude benches in an open-sided church, he sensed happiness and contentment and joy in their singing.

"They're singing about heaven," the translator told Bernie. "Before they received their Bible, they didn't have any hope of heaven. They believed that when they died they were like the insects and animals. Gone. Forgotten. Now they know about Jesus. And they know about heaven. For the first time in history, they have hope."

Watching these people made Bernie think of the heritage from American slaves whose hope in the future was reflected in songs like "Swing low, sweet chariot, comin' for to carry me home" and "This world is not my home, I'm just a'passin' through." He also remembered the poor in Ecuador who attended Bible studies in his home, and whose favorite song was "I've got a home in Gloryland that outshines the sun."

"Maybe the Manobo people have a better grasp on life than we rich, worldly-wise Americans," Bernie said. "They have nothing of this world's goods, yet internally they radiate strength and joy."

Joy in adversity, patience in tribulation, hope in despair—these are the bricks and lumber of Christian character. When the Lord is truly working in our lives, when we accept the cutting and hammering of his craftsmanship, then we'll really know why he said, "I have come that they might have life, and that they might have it more abundantly" (John 10:10, KJV).

Eternal life is not only the destination of heaven. Eternal life also encompasses the *journey* to God's eternal dwelling place. It's life lived in the expectancy that nothing, absolutely nothing, is a mistake when God is in control of our lives. It's the good news that the bad news is not the only news. Sorrow and sin won't win out, for Christ has defeated both through his death and resurrection.

One Woman's Message

It is in dying that we reveal the mettle of our living. When all the dailyness comes down to those last days, hours, and minutes before eternity, we deliver our most unforgettable message about Christianity.

Not all will receive the identical message. Like the proverbial blind men discovering an elephant, those around us will notice and perceive what God has for them alone to learn. Such was the case with Rebecca. At age forty-seven, doctors told her she had cancer and six months to live. She died seven months later.

But in that dying process, she demonstrated that eternal life is lived in the trenches and that knowing Christ makes the difference between defeat and victory.

Her intimate family circle saw one very deep side of this process. Her work colleagues saw another. And those of us who knew her from church saw still another. However we received the message of her life, it affected us.

I remember how I was struck by the radiance in her face, even in those times when I knew she was assaulted by personal and physical sorrows. Yet those trials shaped her character in bringing her to the point of trusting God even while dying.

For most of her life she'd been on the front lines of battle—praying, counseling, helping others in their faith journeys. When cancer came, hundreds in the United States, England, and Paraguay lined up at her battlefront of disease and prayed. But she told her family, "This time the Lord has given me orders to stay at home and stay in peace, to accept whatever he brings. If it's healing, it's to his glory. If it's death, it's still to his glory."

Rebecca's peace and perseverence amazed co-workers as she worked to within a week and a half of her death. She used her illness as a platform to more boldly explain how they, too, could have peace through a relationship with Christ. Even at the end, from her bed, she held three weekly discipling sessions with a new Christian from work.

Then came the last days, and her extended family squeezed into her tiny bedroom, singing hymns and choruses, accompanied by guitars. At one time twenty-five people gathered, just worshiping and expressing their belief that Rebecca's death only meant heaven.

It was into this atmosphere of praise and hope that one friend came to say a final goodbye. The woman's own sister had feared dying throughout her fight with cancer. But Rebecca's peacefulness staggered her. Leaving the house, she turned to a relative and said, "Whatever Rebecca has, I want." He took her aside and explained how to become a Christian.

Rebecca's sister Rachel was awed by Rebecca's courage through the whole ordeal. "From the moment we found out, to her last breath, she showed me that trusting God with all your heart, soul and mind produces courage," Rachel says. "She still had to deal with the consequences of her dying. She had to think about what would happen to her husband, daughters, and grandchildren. Yet she would tell me, 'This is the way God is taking me, and I know he will take care of them.' I never saw her waver. Her courage was such an example to me."

Rebecca's husband Roy says she lived those last days no differently than the majority of the twenty-two years before. But her nearness to eternity had a strong impact on people.

"In those last months," recalls her brother-in-law Dale, "it seemed like she already had one foot in heaven. She lived with such a sense of the reality of the Lord and heaven."

He especially sensed this as they sat near each other at church. "We'd be singing hymns or a praise chorus," Dale says, "and I'd just choke up. The words took on meanings too deep. As I looked over to Rebecca, her hands lifted in praise, I knew she was lost in the Lord's presence in worship."

But Rebecca would have been the first to admit that building character takes time. As a military wife and mother of three daughters, she'd experienced frustrating people and circumstances. True to the principle of Jeremiah 12:5—of running in flat country before tackling the thickets of the Jordan—she'd allowed God to build her obedience and trust.

The key was an ever-deepening faith nurtured by time in prayer and God's Word. Her husband Roy says it was Rebecca's habit to get up early, wrap up in a blanket on the couch in the living room, then read her Bible and pray for more than an hour. Some mornings she'd awaken at three or four o'clock and go to that spot, believing the Lord had roused her to persevere in prayer for special needs. She also spent a hour in devotions before bedtime.

"She loved God like no one I'd known before," says Roy.

In her last months, recalls Dale, "the reality of heaven saturated her words. In her final two weeks on earth, she talked often of two things. One was the importance of showing love to everyone, whether or not they were easy to love. The other was the importance of forgiveness, and how unwillingness to forgive builds barriers between others and Christ."

During her last months, "I fell in love with her again," says her husband Roy. "I had always loved her, but now I finally knew what love really was—totally surrendering myself to her as I saw Rebecca's total surrender to God."

As the cancer progressed, Rebecca's spiritual endurance showed itself in her attitude to embrace life fully. "Every day is a gift from God," she'd say, even of those days when she limped home from work to bed. She loved parties and laughter and focused on joy—and asked her family to do the same. She visited out-of-state relatives, shopped for furniture, and helped her husband start a new business.

"Rebecca and I could have joy," says Roy, "because we'd turned her life over to God, accepting his will as ours. That's all she wanted, to be in the will of God."

And at the end, she reaffirmed her trust that God's way, even through this disease, was best.

"Just a week before we learned of her cancer," recalls Roy, "Rebecca had an overwhelming peace in her body while praying. She said God seemed to say to her, 'Whatever happens, I want you to know that I am in control. I want you just to receive what I have for you.'"

That promise, Roy says, helped her accept that healing was not God's plan for this time. It helped her to pin her hope on God's trustworthiness. It helped her to rejoice that, just beyond death, was heaven.

Rebecca loved crafts and sewing. When I now think about her, I imagine her sharing sewing hints with Joppa's Dorcas, the tailor of Joseph's multi-colored coat, and with my own mother (whose obsession with sewing once caused her to tell the gas station attendant, "Three yards of gas, please").

But I also think of her as reveling in that great, joyful mass of people who find their completion in the presence of God.

Custom Built

"In my Father's house are many rooms," Jesus told us. "If it were not so, I would have told you. I am going there to prepare a place for you" (John 14:2).

Heaven will be custom-built for "community." We get that clue from Jesus' use of the Greek word *monai*, which means "an abode." He used another form of the word in verse 23: "We [My Father and I] will come to him and make our home [*monen*] with him."

Like the dwelling places of Bible times, homes or tents clustered around a well or eating/socializing area, our "abode" in heaven will be uniquely ours, yet offer access to the Throne and hosts of heaven. We'll truly be able to "fix our eyes on Jesus . . . [who] sat down at the right hand of the throne of God" (Heb. 12:2).

I like how Charles Gabriel expressed it in his hymn, "Oh That Will Be Glory":

> Friends will be there I have loved long ago;
> Joy like a river around me will flow;
> Yet, just a smile from my Savior, I know,
> Will through the ages be glory for me.

Spiritually, we're like little children who can hardly wait for Christmas or their birthdays. When mine were younger we'd make a chain with as many links as days to wait. As they cut off a link each day, their excitement mounted.

We need to have that longing for heaven, without demanding that God tell us how many days are left in the meantime. Psalm 90:12 says, "Teach us to number our days aright," but that's so that our spiritual inventory will motivate us toward godliness, "that we may gain a heart of wisdom."

Heaven Will Wait

Heaven can wait for the fullness of time—and Heaven *will* wait. God's time is always right.

There's a picture of that in Revelation 6, where the seals of judgment are broken. It's a dismal setting, the unfolding of a series of disasters on earth. Then attention shifts to heaven as the fifth seal is broken:

> **I** saw under the altar the souls of those who had been slain because of the word of God and the testimony they had maintained. They called out in a loud voice, "How long, Sovereign Lord, holy and true, until you judge the inhabitants of the earth and avenge our blood?" Then each of them was given a white robe, and they were told to wait a little longer, until the number of their fellow servants and brothers who were to be killed as they had been was completed. *Revelation 6:9-11*

Here are saints who died for their faith in Christ. Now they wondered how long evil would prevail on earth. God made no promises. He told them to wait a little longer. He asked them to trust him. Like those saints, we get impatient about God's timetable. But this passage has a great truth, which Robert Coleman helps explain:

> The cry of the martyrs who long for the consummation of history reflects similar feelings in the suffering church on earth. We want to get God's work over in a hurry. In our clouded apprehension of His ways, we

find difficulty in perceiving the vast extent of His world mission and the painstaking process of making a people in His own character, to praise Him forever. And God will not compromise His goals. By placing this song in the narrative of earth's sorrows, God makes us aware that He will not circumvent means in accomplishing His ends. What we consider detours, hardships, even the pangs of death, often are the very things that God uses to confirm us more perfectly to His image. If the Captain of our salvation learned obedience through His sufferings, how can we expect to understand Calvary love on beds of ease?[1]

We may think we're waiting for heaven. *But heaven is waiting for us.* God is not, as many say, getting our mansions ready. *He's getting us ready for our mansions.*

Heaven will be fulfilling. As Charles Wesley wrote, we'll be "lost in wonder, love and praise." We'll serve God (Rev. 22:3) in glad, tireless, fulfilling service. Above all, in heaven we'll see Jesus.

> And I—in righteousness I will see your face; when I awake, I will be satisfied with seeing your likeness. *Psalm 17:15*

> What we will be has not yet been made known. But we know that when he appears, we shall be like him, for we shall see him as he is. *1 John 3:2*

Sometimes I think I couldn't bear to see Jesus. I'd be overwhelmed by my own unholiness in the blinding glare of his perfect holiness. Moses took off his sandals before the Lord's manifestation in a burning bush. Isaiah was so desperate in his holy vision that he cried out, "Woe to me, I am ruined!" (Isa. 6:5).

Yet John gives us hope: "We shall be like him." In our new and changed state, we'll feel comfortable in God's presence.

Gospel songwriter Fanny Crosby sat one night on a hotel porch in Poughkeepsie, New York, after a special camp service. With her was the great Methodist lay evangelist, Dr. L.W. Munhall. The sun was setting, and Dr. Munhall was trying to describe its deepening glory across the skies.

Blind since infancy, Miss Crosby exclaimed, "I cannot see the sunset, but someday I shall see my Savior face to face." That comment gave birth to her hymn, "Saved By Grace." Its third stanza says:

> Some day, when fades the golden sun
> Beneath the rosy-tinted west,
> My blessed Lord will say, "Well done!"
> And I shall enter into rest.
> And I shall see Him face to face,
> And tell the story—saved by grace.[2]

Until that time, the God of the Universe is at work among us. We're in that workroom whose door reads "Patience." Inside, the clutter of living pulls us through experiences and relationships that deepen our capacities for longsuffering, forbearance, endurance and perseverance.

Most of all, they teach us to trust.

Several years ago a young Dutch-born woman named Inka, married to an American, received a little ceramic plaque containing a Dutch prayer. The poem began, "I lay the names of my children in Thy hands," and the author emphasized committing her children to God, trusting him to keep them even if she had to let them go.

A few months later Inka was diagnosed with liver cancer and died, leaving a husband and three small children.

A few years later Inka's husband remarried. The new mother for Inka's children was one of my graduate school friends, Cindy Secrest McDowell. As Cindy unpacked one day after a cross-country move, she came across the plaque with its translation on the back in Inka's handwriting. In the reverence of that moment, she realized how Inka was literally called upon to lay the names of her three children in the Lord's hands.

This is a picture of what God is asking of every one of us. He wants us to place in his hands those relationships and possessions that become precious to us. As he searches our priorities, he asks difficult questions:

- Are you impatient with others when God is patient with you?

- Are you impatient with trials when you know God is building you into the person you were meant to be?

- Are you impatient for heaven or just impatient with earth?

When we've reached the point of true trust, of honestly and totally accepting his rulership in our lives, of relinquishing all for his best, the next door will be opened to Glory.

I've learned *not* to pray for patience. Instead, I ask God to teach me to be faithful. We need to pray that God's construction program will build us into whole persons, un-ruffled by circumstances and balanced in temperament. We need to pray to be holy people, aware of our inadequacy apart from Jesus Christ, but able to endure, persevere, and trust through the spiritual strength he provides.

That lapel button I found in the garage is right: Please be patient. Before we know it, God will be finished with us, and the struggle will be worth it all.

Something to Build On

1. What instruction is given to believers in Hebrews 6:12? How can you work that out in your life?

2. What, for you, is the hardest aspect of the teaching we find in James 5:7-8?

3. What encouragement can you take from 1 Corinthians 15:58?

4. What will we do in heaven?

   > Matthew 19:28
   > 1 Corinthians 6:2-3
   > Revelation 14:13

And we pray this in order that you may live a life worthy of the Lord and may please him in every way, bearing fruit in every good work, growing in the knowledge of God, being strengthened with all power according to his glorious might so that you may have great endurance and patience, and joyfully giving thanks to the Father, who has qualified you to share in the inheritance of the saints in the kingdom of light.—Colossians 1:10-12

Notes

Introduction

1. Paul E. Billheimer, *Don't Waste Your Sorrows* (Fort Washington, Penn.: Christian Literature Crusade, and Minneapolis: Bethany House, 1977), p. 44.

Chapter 1

1. Quoted by Philip Yancey in *Disappointment With God* (Grand Rapids, Mich.: Zondervan, 1988), p. 157.

Chapter 2

1. J. I. Packer, "A Bad Trip," *Christianity Today*, March 7, 1986, p. 12.

2. Donald E. Demaray, *Laughter, Joy and Healing* (Grand Rapids, Mich.: Baker Book House, 1986), p. 39.

3. Oswald Chambers, *My Utmost For His Highest*, (Dodd Mead & Co., 1935; Oswald Chambers Publications Assoc., 1963), p. 243.

4. George Sanville, *Forty Gospel Hymn Stories* (Winona Lake: Rodeheaver-Hall Mack Co., 1943), p. 20.

Chapter 3

1. Charles Spurgeon, edited by William Hillyer, *Great Verses From the Psalms* (Grand Rapids, Mich.: Zondervan, 1976), p. 57.

2. Ibid., p. 57.

3. James Bishop, *The Spirit of Christ in Human Relationships*, (Grand Rapids, Mich.: Zondervan, 1968), p. 24.

4. C. S. Lewis, *The Problem of Pain*, 2nd ed. (New York: Macmillan, 1962), p. 93.

Chapter 4

1. Jerry and Mary White, *Friends and Friendship* (Colorado Springs: NavPress, 1982), p. 91.

Chapter 5

1. Kevin Leman, *Measuring Up* (Old Tappan, N.J.: Fleming H. Revell, 1988), pp. 165–166.

Chapter 6

1. A. W. Tozer, "God Is Easy to Live With," *The Root of the Righteous* (Camp Hill, Penn.: Christian Publications, 1986), p. 16.
2. R. C. Sproul, *One Holy Passion* (Nashville: Thomas Nelson, 1987), pp. 166–167.
3. Dietrich Bonhoeffer, *Life Together*, (New York: Harper & Row, 1954), p. 86.

Chapter 7

1. Oswald Chambers, *My Utmost For His Highest*, p. 129.
2. Andrew Murray, *Waiting on God* (Chicago: Moody Press, n.d.), pp. 59–60.

Chapter 8

1. Charles F. Pfeiffer, *The Epistle to the Hebrews* (Chicago: Moody Press, 1962), p. 107.

2. James Moffat, *A New Translation of the Bible*, (New York: HarperCollins, 1935), p. 284.

3. Carroll F. Hunt, *From the Claws of the Dragon* (Grand Rapids, Mich.: Zondervan, 1988), p. 52.

4. Ibid., p. 65.

Chapter 9

1. Harold Fickett, *Faith That Works*, (Ventura, Calif.: Regal Books, 1972), p. 10.

Chapter 10

1. Robert Coleman, *Songs of Heaven* (Old Tappan, N.J.: Fleming H. Revell, 1980), p. 74.

2. George Sanville, *Forty Gospel Hymn Stories* (Winona Lake: Rodeheaver-Hall Mack Co., 1943), p. 36.